P9-BJW-405

The Girl

Novel by
Meridel Le Sueur

The Girl

Novel by
Meridel Le Sueur

Revised Edition 1990

West End Press

*To Robert Aaron Brown
and that dark city of St. Paul.*

*And for Natalie, Anna, Bernice, Gladys, Doris, Sara,
all living, all real, all in need.*

O that my head was water and mine eyes a flood of tears that I might weep day and night for the slain of the daughters of my people.

Is there no balm in Gilead? Is there no physician? Is not the health of the daughters of my people recovered?

They are broken with a great breath, with a grievous blow.

Through all the land the wounded shall groan.

The harvest is passed and the summer is ended and we are not saved.

The land is desolate because of the presence of the oppressor.

For the hurt of the daughters of my people, I am hurt.

Jeremiah (adapted)

The following portions of this novel have been reprinted separately as short stories:

"They Follow Us Girls" in *Anvil*, July–Aug. 1935.
"Salvation Home" in *New Masses*, Jan. 10, 1939.
"Sure, Honey!" in *New Anvil*, June–July 1939.
"I'm Going I Said" in *New Masses*, Jan. 9, 1940.
"Father of the Earth" in *The Fountain*, March 1942.
"O Prairie Girl Be Lonely" in *New Caravan*, 1945.

"The Story and the Living: Meridel Le Sueur's *The Girl*" by Joseph Napora, © 1982 by Cardinal Press. Reprinted by permission.

"The Book's Progress: The Making of *The Girl*" by John Crawford, © 1990 by John Crawford.

Drawing for *The Girl* by Bill Norman (1939). Courtesy of the Minnesota Historical Society.

First printing 1978; second printing 1979; third printing 1981; fourth printing (WEP/MEP edition) 1982; fifth printing 1985; sixth printing 1986.

Revised edition — first printing 1990; second printing 1992.

Typography, design, and production by Michael Reed of Prototype, Albuquerque, New Mexico.

ISBN 0-931122-56-2
$8.95

West End Press • Box 27334 • Albuquerque, New Mexico 87125

1

Saturday was the big day at the German Village, where I was lucky to get a job in those bad times, and Clara and I were the only waitresses and had to be going up and down from the bar to the bootleg rooms upstairs. My mama had told me that the cities were Sodom and Gomorrah, and terrible things could be happening to you, which made me scared most of the time.

I was lucky to get the job after all the walking and hunting Clara and I had been doing. I was lucky to have Clara showing me how to wander on the street and not be picked up by plainclothesmen and police matrons. They will pick you up, Clara told me, and give you tests and sterilize you or send you to the woman's prison. I liked to be with Clara and hear about it, and now with Belle, who with Hoinck her husband and Ack his brother ran the German Village. It wasn't German but lots of even stylish people came there after hours for the bootleg Belle and Hoinck made.

Clara told me all about what was going on up there and it scared me— the men who came in the back alley door and went past the bar and upstairs scared me. Clara told me about Ganz, who brought in bootleg from Dakota and paid protection for the place. I shivered when he passed me. And Clara would take my place when Belle told me to take them beer, because she said she could "field" them better when they tried to make a home run or a strike, with their too-free paws. Sometimes I didn't even know the words Clara spoke. I had a lot to learn, Clara said.

You're sure hot on that Butch, Clara nudged me. He won't be here tonight till later on. Saturday nights him and Hoinck take a turkish bath and get spruced up. You stir the Booya, she says to me, and watch your Ps and Qs. That there Butch is a dangerous cat.

Belle was pretty famous with her Saturday night Booya. It's an elegant stew of chicken and veal and beef and every kind of vegetable and you cook it all night and all day very, very slow and it gets to smelling even out on the streets and the cats look in the window.

Pretty good, Clara says, as I carried four mugs of Booya dancing neat around drunken people, but I keep watching for Butch to come in the door, for the sight of him seemed to make me light up like a wick caught fire.

I kept as close to Clara as I could. Something was in her so sure as if she knew everything I would never know. She made the hollowness of my flesh fill with people and she believed in love and everything comes to those who wait, kid—you would get anything you hankered for, she said, if you'd believe and keep it in the mind's eye. Stirring the Booya pot so it wouldn't stick, Clara said, you might find that rich guy here you know, or a movie director or a talent scout who is just looking for your face, and modeling is good too.

O, there's a rainbow for everyone, she said, a pot of gold and the dice falling right. Just keep your eyes peeled, kid, and shine up to them. O, Clara was so pretty with a little heart-shaped face and a white soft skin she greased every night.

The place was a whiz that Saturday night. The whole place was really lit up by Belle. She must have been a beauty once. She still was, on Saturday nights. She's so big, with dyed red hair and white skin and her eyes made up so they glittered, and you could hear her laughing upstairs and downstairs and even out in the back, where the bootleg was put into bottles and men came in the alley door and passed their money in and put the bottle in their overcoat pockets and disappeared. And when I'd go to fill up the bottles Ack would try to put his arms around me but Clara had shown me how to dodge and not make anybody mad.

I liked to see Belle at the bar shaking dice and the big cat Susybelly in a big bow by the register, with a piggy bank beside her full of money from the bets being put down on how many cats she would pop. There was another pot on how many girl or boy cats. The pot was getting mighty big. Belle would horse around with the men. I never saw anything like it. It is good business, Clara says—Belle is a mighty good smart woman but she drinks too much. I would watch them laughing and Belle would playfully tickle them and they would try to feel her up or slap her on the buttocks.

Their German band which was Irish would begin a polka, looking mighty smart in front of the lattice with painted roses which hid the biffies with the signs saying Fritz and Frau. You can win this and the chocolate's on me, the player said. I like nuts, Belle shouted, and the whole bar roared and sneezed through their noses and yelled—O Lord God, she likes nuts, and people in the booths stood up to see.

Amelia was there, having a Saturday night beer, with her black linoleum bag of stuff to tell you what was happening and how you must come and be with others who needed your help.

She said hello to Clara, and, who's the new girl? and Clara said, O, a virgin from the country scared of her shadow. And Amelia said so kindly, welcome girl, and Clara said, her mama told her the city was a wicked place and she'd fall into hell. I left my mama in Cleveland, Ohio, and when I went back she was gone and the house was empty, she said.

Come down with us, Amelia said.

Where is that? I said.

The Workers Alliance, she said, where the workers is all together and don't have to be afraid.

My mama had eight children, Clara said, they took four away from her and I run away to something bigger and better.

Belle shouts out, take the old lady a beer.

No listen, Hoinck said, I told you about the handouts.

You shut up and leave her alone, you son of satan. She's gonna have whatever she likes. You come here anytime and rest your feet, Amelia, like I say. She understands me, she thinks we are all important.

Everyone is important, Amelia says, and I am thinking she looks like mama, like she has carried a lot and fought a lot and endured a lot.

Why sure, Clara says, knowledge is power, the early bird gets the worm.

What you got there in your bag, Amelia?

That's heavy, Amelia says, that's literature.

I got to catch up on my reading, Clara says.

Can I have one? I says, reaching for the leaflet. The big letters say, Don't starve—Organize.

Belle shouts. Four upstairs. Shake your ass.

I wanted to ask her more but I had to look at the doors opening in the cold steam and no Butch. You think something happened to him? I shouted to Clara , as we ran past each other with the mugs of beer. She shook her head laughing, her little mouth like a hungry rabbit's. Passing me she yelled, No news is good news. He'll turn up, the bad penny he is.

It got pretty noisy and crowded. I never saw anything like it. Belle was keeping it all going, laughing and yelling and shooting the dice. She calls me over. Ganz asked for you. He wants you to bring him his Booya.

I don't want to go, I said. Clara said she would go.

Why baby, Belle says, he asked for you. Why you're *in*.

Clara punched me in the ribs. Go on, kid.

I'm afraid, I don't like him.

You don't have to like him, Belle said. He gives this place protection. He can butter your bread. The cops don't bother us on account of him. He could give you anything.

I wished he'd ask for me, Clara said. I know, kid, you feel all lighted up if Butch should come in the door but you need butter on your bread and cream in your coffee. Butch can't give you anything but love, baby— here angel, take this to Ganz, and she gave me the bowl of Booya. Look forward baby, she said, look up. Be like me, always looking to a bright future and peace.

Belle shouted, If he gets fresh call out. A horse on me. She shook the dice. Will I ever be easy with a man like Belle and Clara? I thought. What do they know I don't know? Clara told me men cry for it. She said she was glad she was a girl so men would cry for what she had and shake all over. She said about Butch's brother Bill that he wanted her, can't get her off his mind, dreams about her. He keeps kissing her, she says, and crying and trembling. I felt I would like to make Butch cry and tremble and then comfort him.

I tried not to shake and spill the Booya and there was Ganz and he got up and tried to put his arm around me. I ducked with the Booya.

Remember me? he said.

No I don't know you, I said, your name is Ganz.

Well that'll be a starter, he said. You might as well know I keep this place going. I nodded, and he began to tell me how good he was, how he knocked out Four Round Hogan once. He said he gave him a good beating because he got mad and when he got mad at anybody he didn't know what he did—he was a fierce one and pretty tough. He said it wouldn't hurt a girl to be nice to him, though, he was very nice when he was nice. I could hardly sit beside him.

3

I could just see the opening door when Clara came in to bring the shots of whiskey and maybe she came in oftener than she had to. She'd roll her eye and shake her head like signals, but I didn't know what they meant.

O, I wanted to see Butch and his brother Bill come in and I thought I would just get up and run downstairs. I was scared to see him too. He was sweet on me, Clara said. He was smooth as silk to look at. He and his brother Bill, smart as whips and walked and strutted, their shoulders going down to their hips and narrow sleek heads, and Butch looked smooth and sleepy as if about to spring like a cat.

There was a kind of roar in the place, a hum. I felt hot and strange and the sweat ran down my armpits clean down my side and I could hardly see through the smoke and a kind of funny light.

Then something kind of exploded in my eyes and I saw him come in through the steam, uncover his black sleek head. Clara stuck her head in nodding, and I got up and ran to the open door and down the stairs and I looked at his long face lean like a fox. I was scared. I couldn't see very well. I was shaking in all my bones. There was danger in the way he walked towards me, his hands out, his face above me. How you doin' baby? he cried, how you doin' tonight?

2

Clara passing me with five mugs of beer had cried —Happy baby? There they are, Bill and Butch, the two slick cats. Don't say I didn't warn you.

Butch took over the bar and I tried to stay downstairs so I could just look and see him. It was then I couldn't help hearing Belle and Hoinck, getting the bootleg for the late customer.

We got to decide, Belle said, listen darling listen Hoinck we never done no big robbery like this before.

Hoinck said—When the trap snaps does the rabbit argue?

O Hoinck save the best stuff, O we got our luck, they still roll for us those babies still roll.

Sure honey. Here's down the hatch. Shake 'em, shake those dice. Snake eyes! Snake eyes!

Butch leaned over me and I felt like a bird on a barbecue spike. See those muscles baby, I worked in a foundry when I was fifteen. If the depression hadn't hit us I'd be foreman right now. They want me back.

He made me feel his muscle. Gee, I said. I had to run to the booths. When I came back for five beers he said, drawing down the draft beer— Stick with me baby I'll show you everything. I'll show you how to be winning. You're a shy thing, too young to leave your mother, what's that about baking a cherry pie? . . .

I could hardly wait to get back with orders. I could see the back of his head in the mirror like a fox in a thicket. When it got crowded Bill came back to help him and Clara and I would meet waiting for the beer and Clara was flirting with Bill.

Ask Bill, Butch said, he'll tell you I'm a natural winner.

Don't let him give you any crap, Bill said.

I like to beat, I like to win, Butch said.

Sure, Bill said. Beating's everything, everything there is.

Clara said, Every cloud has a silver lining.

Bill said, Gold, baby. We're sure gold. We're natural winners, ain't we Butch?

We're natural winners. You should have seen us playing ball. Our old man didn't want us to play ball on Sundays. We used to pray that ball right over the home plate. I used to say to that ball, Go on baby, do good.

I'll roll 'em with you boy. Come over on the outside. Connect.

Stand by me baby and they'll roll for me. Muscle and prayer and a girl like you and what can stop you. Know what I mean.

The good things will all come to you, Clara says.

Clara knows what to want, Bill says.

What? I cried. What?

O you sweet baby, what?

There's winning and the good feeling it gives you, and love of a good man, Clara cries, who has a house in Florida and a swimming pool. I think two bedrooms is enough.

5

And a girl who likes it, Butch said touching my arms as I picked up the white foamed beer mugs. Take it easy, he laughs, you're spilling the profits. My mother is screwy too.

You're making fun, I cried.

Take it easy, Clara says, but take it.

Every time I'd come to the station Butch would be talking. The machine is a beautiful thing, he said once. Did you know I put plows together, yes sir welding, a sweet job and you saw the whole plow when it was put together and you felt proud. And later he said, Yes sir, I worked in a mine nine hundred feet underground and you didn't know night from day. And Bill said, Would you hit a woman? Butch said winking at me, I might pull her eyebrows down a little. It ain't enough, Bill said, you got to knock the holy vinegar out of her.

O Lord, men, Belle said patting Susybelly who was acting funny. Are they telling you some cock and bull story? Never believe a word they say.

Amelia came over and looked at Susybelly. It's her time, she said.

Wouldn't you know? Belle said lifting her up, what a showoff. Picked the busiest night of the week. O.K. baby, give.

Clara said, Look at that now. Cats get better care than humans. She got a cup of milk a day. Help her, can't you?

Everybody's got to do it alone, Belle says putting Suzy back in her box. I could see she was laboring to bring them out. Already I saw the little white bag and a curled cat inside.

Is she really popping? Butch was peering down into the box, Give me six Suzy, give me those boxcars.

There she comes, everyone shouted, and I could see them putting up more bets. Seven come eleven, five studs. . . . How about one on the house, Belle? Don't have a birth here every day.

I could see Amelia push the first wet cat over and press down for the next.

Boy, Butch said, she got it down machine gun. She can count. Three four five, he counted laughing.

She's a female like us, Amelia said, she don't know the father, she gives all she's got to make them come out whole healthy full of seed. Hold the light over closer.

Everyone was gathered round looking into the box and the light swung a little and Butch was leaning over the bar like at a game counting and laughing. There it is, six—that's my number Suzy, that's it. There was a groan and then a shout and screams, Wait—wait—don't count the jackpot yet, sure enough another one there it is, lucky seven . . . round on the house for Susybelly!

Yes, Amelia said wiping her hands and straightening her funny black hat that sat on her bun. One thing comes out of another one. I say the same with society, one gives birth to another, that's the way it is. One dies, another is born. . . .

Hurray, three cheers and down the hatch for birth, Bill and Butch poured out the moon into the whiskey glasses, held up and downed and held again.

I saw Amelia put her heavy sack on her shoulder, which seemed to slope from her carrying. Girl, she said to me as I helped her, Girl I had six children. Yes six, and I saw in her eyes they were all gone, I saw in her eyes a terrible suffering. And once I saw this in mama's eyes although she never had said a word. Oh mama, I cried, and put my arms around Amelia and she seemed very small and thin and I hated to see her go out alone in the cold night.

There were shouts and laughter as they divided up the piggy bank. They couldn't find out which were male cats and which females. That comes later, Belle said. I wanted to stay near Butch who was talking a lot and laughing and giving double shots.

Close your mouth, Clara said once. He ain't a vision.

I covered my mouth.

It wasn't no time till Belle was crying—Closing time. All out. You hear me folks.

A cop was standing by the door. Ganz was standing at the top of the stairs.

They put on a good show. Don't throw us out on the streets. We're just warming up in the bullpen, they cried.

The customers all filed out past the cop and Belle locked the front door after I thought Ganz had nodded to the cop.

Butch was pretty merry and he danced me around and Bill danced Clara. I never been so close to him before. He said in my ear, I'm gonna buy a service station of my own. Be my own man. You better go with me I'm a winner.

I felt like my mama, mute, I couldn't speak. I couldn't say anything. Clara saw I was just grinning and made a face at me.

There was knocks on the alley door and half the customers trooped back in and sat at the booths and you had to serve them again, this time mostly bootleg and bottles to shore them up for morning. Ganz is upstairs leaning over, talking to Hoinck and Ack and I get nervous when Butch joins them and how they are passing a bottle around between them.

I can see Belle with her great red head down on her big arms. Clara is smooching with Bill in a booth.

I was tired, dead tired. I put my head down on my arms. I cold see Butch's serious fox head leaning in to hear Ganz.

And I went to sleep.

3

Things got to be very strong between Butch and me.

Wandering around with Clara down by the levee, stopping where a new building was going up and shouting at the men because Clara says she always likes to talk to men who work hard, and listen to them—I don't know what Clara knows. I would only be able to talk and laugh and escape them very often.

Clara says everybody can get along if they try. She has a box she puts her money in but it is empty most of the time what with sickness and the clothes she has to have. She says though she will have enough money someday, and she will get married and sing in the choir and play bridge on Sundays with the best people. Or she might get a typewriter business in a swanky hotel and wear black dresses with white collars and cuffs and see that everyone comes to work on time. Or a tea shop is a good thing and some people rent a whole house and rent out rooms to the best people and sleep until ten.

She wants only peace and gets only trouble, she says, and she wants everything she sees. She calls it hankering. She has more kinds of hankering than I ever saw. She says you can't make enough on any job to get what you are needing. Clara would tell me her life while we were wandering and hankering.

She says her mother worked in a restaurant till she had a boy baby and they fired her and her father a cabinet maker lost his job and the social worker took the baby away, and her mother went to Buffalo and her father out west looking for a job. She had had Clara in Buffalo and used to leave her locked in a room and go out to feed her. She worked in a mill until the father came back and she got another baby and they fired her. That's just women's luck, Clara said. That's the way a woman always gets it. She hitchhiked to another city so they wouldn't take Clara away from her.

She married a guy but he beat Clara so her mother ran again carrying *his* child and she just clung onto Clara. But Clara passed for older and worked in a sweatshop when she was twelve.

She doesn't like any of it. She just goes along in her own way spinning out of herself like a spider. She is always looking to the future. She is always looking to a bright future and peace.

She taught me to stand by the University Club when the rich men come out. It's all right, she told me, if you are always looking for something better. You meet nice men and you close your eyes and think how someday you will have Irish tablecloths and peasant pottery and a pew in church and dress up and go every Sunday because you haven't had to hustle on Saturday nights.

And I told her about my family how my papa thinks everybody done him wrong and he beat us all, beat my mama too. He just beat us because he saw what we wanted and couldn't give. How we moved from one house and city to another in the Midwest, always trying to get into something bigger and better, trading something, moving and how once we traded a farm with only plum trees on it so we moved again, us kids sitting on the heaps of stuff, and mama crying and praying.

And we put our arms around each other, our lives being so the same. You love him? Clara said about Butch. That's bad. It'll come to no good.

We are going to have a service station on County Road B, I said.

Say no kiddin'. Ain't love grand. I'm going to join the Book of the Month Club. I bet you get married before me and I got the nightgowns saved. I got my fortune told at the Russian Tea Shop. There are a lot of roads going different directions, she says, and love at the end of every road. There was a bird. O kid, she cried, we deserve it all. Do you think I'll fry in hell? I am good. We are good, kid. You got to feel decent. You go on kid, get up in the world and leave me down here.

I won't leave you honey, I cried, feeling her body so thin and her hungry breath.

I listened about men from Belle while I wandered with Clara. Clara's been twice to the house of correction and she says you learn a lot about how not to get screwed there. Belle says this is a rotten stinking world and for women it is worse, and with your insides rotting out of you and men at you day and night and the welfare workers following you and people having to live off each other like rats. It's covered with slime, she says. I wouldn't bring up no kids in it. She says she had thirteen abortions. Clara is very cheerful, cutting out pictures from the magazines showing elegant houses and drapes and furniture and stuff for the baby room and maid's room, all the best stuff, but at night she cries thinking she is going to hell because of what she does with men, but Belle says we are in hell right now and there isn't a God who would make men and women wanting what they want and then stick them in a hell after they've done it.

Between Butch and me it got to be very strong so that I looked for him in every bar and employment place. It was like he was a magnet pulling me. It was exciting and powerful and frightening. He was after me too and when he found me I would run, or be petrified, just standing in front of him like a zany. And he told me not to be wandering with Clara to the Marigold where we danced with strangers. He said he would knock the shit out of me. Which made me shake and tremble, but it was better than being a husk full of suffering and not knowing why.

I had been looking for him all afternoon. It was Saturday too. Nothing was open on Saturday, besides he had said that he and Bill were going to start Monday at the foundry. Amelia said there was a strike there, but they were going anyway they said.

Clara says, Just wait at the Village and he'll turn up. She says, We got what they want and they'll give anything to get it. You got to use your wits, she says.

Then before seven, sure enough before I knew it, there was Butch, quick as a fox walking like a slanting ship in a storm, blowing in the front door and acting like he didn't see me, and three men moved over at the bar and he began shooting the bones and I just stood looking at the way his back was so smooth and silky going to his very small hips. At last he turned holding out a hand to me.

He took thirty cents off of me, he said, can you match that.

O Butch, I said, I'm glad you come, I waited so long for you.

There you go, on my neck. I get laid in lavender everywhere I go. A beer Clara, on the double. There you go blaming me.

I'm not blaming you, I said. Why am I so stupid.

That's right jump on me. Well I got a job, me and Bill, beginning Monday.

I didn't say, There's a strike there.

Listen baby, I can take care of myself I been getting jobs since I got out of didies. I don't need any skirt to tell me the ropes. Hey where's the beer? You got any money? My credit's kaput here.

I paid Clara and sat near him in the booth. I felt so light and warm near him. I know, I said, You'll always be winning.

He looked sad suddenly. We ain't even got a place to go. Even if you would go with me we ain't got a gopher hole, a fox hole, we got nothing.

I got three dollars coming. O we'll get something, I said. I'm saving my money for the service station. You'll see.

O for Christ's sake, he said, let's get where other people are worse off anyway, baby.

4

We went upstairs. Hoinck was very drunk and they were all sitting around the table in the middle of the joint. We went over and they made room for us. I sat by Belle and she put her arm around me. Hoinck was telling about how they all went to Belle's sister's funeral and they only had one dress suit and they shook for it and Ack won and it was too big for him and Hoinck had to go in his old clothes. They got pie-eyed and went to the swanky undertaking parlors where she was supposed to be and they wouldn't let them in. Belle got mad and began shouting and putting on a show and grabbed the phone, and Ack fell downstairs into the morgue, dress suit and all. It turned out, Hoinck said, that Belle hadn't seen this sister anyway for twelve years and didn't know what she looked like and she wasn't dead anyway!

Everybody laughed a lot. I never thought any of Hoinck's stories were funny. He said, Belle here is some woman. I got me some woman. She took the rap for me once when I forged a check, and she had thirteen abortions. I give her a spoonful of turpentine with sugar and it'll loosen anything, ain't that so Belle? Everybody laughed some more. Belle seemed to like it too. I didn't think any of it was funny.

I used to be a regular nut, Acks says, so did Hoinck here, we were raised like good Baptists. We belonged to more churches, didn't we Hoinck?

Hoinck said, There was a time when we just about kept the churches in this country going! Every cent we had over food and lodging went to the churches. Why I used to preach on the street myself.

Ack said, They used to call us Peter and Paul.

Hoinck said, Me and Belle here we'd pray, get down alongside the bed and pray until we dropped off to sleep right there on our knees. Why we even spoke in tongues once when we got the holy spirit.

They all hooted at that. Butch said, Drink up honey. You'll feel better. Here's down the old hatch.

I drank some beer. I did feel better. I did feel good and all I could see was Butch and he held my hand and some of it got to be funny.

An old man kept butting in singing. He said he was lonely because his wife was in Rochester. A fat Greek named Artzybetsoff. He said his wife was a Bohemian and very handsome and it was bad to lose your wife even for one night. Yes, the old man said, and began to sing again.

Tell about speaking in tongues, Belle said to Hoinck.

Yes sir, he said, we could tell we were doing it by the way the words were separated, it was tongues sure enough! Belle here spoke for one solid hour it's a fact! It came on her when she was kneeling. I was driving a truck then and I had to go out on my run but I asked the old lady to pray for me so I would get it too. She prayed all night. I kept my mind on it too all the time I was driving. Sure enough I was just untying my shoes in Cincinnati, dead tired, when I got it! I spoke for forty minutes switching from one tongue to another without no stopping for breath.

Everybody howled. It's the God's truth, Belle said laughing.

But we're all done with that now, Hoinck said. It was when the worst part of the depression first banged us up and I couldn't get a thing. Yes sir, I made doll furniture and Belle here used to peddle it from door to door. I helped the churches all that time I thought they ought to help me. I went to the parson, the assistant parson, the deacons, the choir leader, and they looked at me with fishes' faces.

They told me to go to charities. Well I ain't never going to live off no charity. I ain't never going to do it. To hell with those snooty spinsters poking their noses in my business. Well after I left the church I got a course from some magazine, a course in psychology. You all probably heard about it. I never heard of it until I seen this piece in the paper. Well it made a new man out of me. I learned that thought is all-powerful. You can make anything so by believing it's so. You make your own good and cure your own evil.

Well, Butch said, Hoinck, think us another round.

A round on the house, Belle yelled.

Yes sir, Hoinck went on, you don't need anybody to do it for you. You do it in your own mind. It's just the opposite of all that religion I believed in.

Yes sir, Butch says, you worked yourself up to an extreme state of poverty!

Everybody laughed.

You can laugh, Hoinck says, but it works for you. Why I used to give Ack here an awful tongue lashing every time I caught him looking at the pictures outside a burlesque show. Now I go to one every time I can. Everything is good. Before me and my old woman used to cry and pray every time our flesh was weak. Now she's like me. We love each other up whenever we feel like it and never worry. Everything is good.

Amen, Butch said and we all laughed. It seemed very funny now.

Beer is good, the old man said, when it's good beer!

Then the Greek had to show a picture of his brother who was a fighter and who died in an automobile accident. In the picture you could see him sitting with his shanks apart, very greased and his muscles bulging.

Belle said to Butch, Did you find a job today? I saw you with such a face on you this morning. How will you get a job looking like that? So black like this—she put her thumbs in her cheeks and pulled her mouth down. That is no way to get a job. No, you have to look cheerful, like this, and she pulled her thumbs up so her eyes disappeared in her fat cheeks.

I don't feel cheerful, Butch said. I am not cheerful.

Who is? You have to look like it, that is all.

Well, I won't, Butch said.

What is the matter? Belle said. She was always so full of such good advice women want to be giving men that they never take. What is the matter? What would you like to do? We'll concentrate on it.

Butch swore—Mind your own business for God's sake.

It is my business. I don't like to see a man go to waste.

I want a job, Butch said, Jesus Christ, I want a lot of things. I'm full as a tick of what I want.

Sure, she said, certainly, I know what a young man wants. It is awful, no work for men. Women know it too. When there is no work for men, women are in for a bad time too. It is terrible for women.

O, to hell with women!

You can't say that. When women go to hell men go along, that's the way it is. What we should do, Belle says, is get out of there, get away. Look! There is Canada and the wild lands.

Yeah, Butch said, that's what I'd like to do. There is too many after one job in a city.

Hoinck says, The hunting there in the morning! You can shoot into the air and even with half an eye bring down a duck!

Yes, Belle says, that's the life.

We all put in our two cents' worth, about homesteading, about land still to be had, and land that is turning back to the state for the taxes.

No, no, Belle says, that's dead land. You have to have new land, new land, the farther the better. We got to have something new now. Ah! Canada! That's what I love and there are the little violets up there, yes, and what are those other flowers with deep throats?

You can get land, Hoinck says, and live cheap as dirt. A man doesn't have to do a thing but put out his traps.

You'd all get sick on fresh air, Ack says.

Let's take our car, Belle cries, let's drive up there. We could go on a vacation and find some land and then the others could come after.

It's a go! Butch shouts. Good. It's a go. Look, he says wild-looking, look honey, we'll do it, get away from everything. Look honey, that's our out. Are you game?

Yes, O, yes, I said. Anything, Butch, anything!

Gee, you're swell. Gee, honey, I'm crazy about you, you're so sweet. We'll have some land, we'll get you fat with roses in your cheeks and then we can have that ballplayer, fat and sassy.

Belle threw her arms around us laughing, throwing back her wild head. We'll go in my car.

Our car, Hoinck roared.

Our car, Belle cries, trying to reach his face to kiss him. We'll all go in our car.

Will you honey? Butch says.

Sure, sure, Butch, I said. Sure!

I knew that car wouldn't cross the Mississippi.

5

That whole weekend was spooky. Like waves that don't break. Like something was coming towards us all you couldn't name or see. On Sunday it was like we all had to gather together at the German Village. Even the customers begged to be let in at the alley door, begging for a bottle to get over Sunday.

Sunday, Belle says, is a voodoo day. Sunday is the entrance into hell. It's the day bootleg was made for. Let the poor bastards in. Give them a snort for God's sake. And they all sat around drooping like wet buzzards.

Butch and Bill hung in there like they was afraid to go to the foundry the next morning, and they turned off the radio so they wouldn't hear that the governor had called in the state militia to protect the scabs.

Why, the Gov says that it's patriotic to keep the foundry going, Bill said, and he and Butch looked so much alike, grinning and bragging.

You think you should scab? I said.

Why, the Gov says it's a wildcat. They're giving a bonus.

Say listen, Bill said, Butch and me are an unbeatable team. We been playing and winning together since we pulled up our didies and said howdy, ain't that so, Brother Butch?

It sure is so, Brother Bill, Butch said, and they put their sleek black heads together. Sure we're winners sister, we're strong. We're good. It ain't natural we shouldn't be winning. I like to beat everybody in the world.

You do? I said to Butch.

Sure, beating's everything. Everything there is. Do you know winning is better than anything, than anything at all. When I used to play baseball I liked to beat. I was a good player. Jesus, my old man didn't want me to play baseball on Sunday. I used to pray to that ball, yeah man, I'd pray plenty. I used to say to that ball, Go on baby, do good! Yes, I got to be better than anybody, better than anybody at all. When you play ball you pray, that's the way I pray now, to be better than anybody. When you play ball you pray, those balls come over on the inside and connect. That's what I'm going to do. Let it come to me world, and connect.

O, sure! I couldn't help laughing.

That's the way I used to do it and O, it was sweet to me too sometimes, just like you could be honey. Twenty-one strikeouts one day, would you believe it? That's no horse feathers. Closed both eyes and wanged and it went over!

I never heard anything like this. Men are funny.

Yeah, he said, muscle and prayer and who can stop you? Luck's got to be with you and a girl too. One comes over straight and in close and I wind her up and put it down so they don't know where it's coming from. Know what I mean?

No, I said, it's Greek to me.

Jesus, he says, don't you know baseball either?

No, I says, not very much.

Gee, he says, there's another thing I got to teach you. I got lots to teach you baby, and you get over being so scared and you'll learn what people want in this world. There's plenty good things to want.

What? I said.

O plenty, Lord, plenty.

What?

There's winning all the time and the good feel it gives you and doing things, you know with the English on it, know what I mean? And driving a fast car. And having a girl who likes it and knows how to do it.

I could feel the bright blood in me.

It takes guts, he said, that's what it is, to go through the night. You got to be tough and strong alone.

I don't like it alone, I said. I don't want to be alone. I want to be with others.

He looked at me. Gee, women are funny eggs, he said. My mother's a screwy dame too!

I felt I said the wrong thing now.

You know what it is? My mother remembers only the good things that happened to her.

Like what?

O, like she remembers my father is still alive. She thinks her own mother, who's been rotting in her grave twenty years, is coming down to breakfast. She remembers us kids like we was still young. She still thinks she lives in the best house we had once with five rooms. There isn't a better woman on earth than my mother but she's bats. All women are bats.

It looked like he wanted to tell me everything again, how he worked in a mine, and how he worked assembling snow plows for seventy cents an hour and you got to put together a whole machine and see it work and everything. I didn't know men like that.

Listen, honey, he said, you be good to me.

I am good to you.

You be good to me and I'll go places, nothing can stop me. We can have everything.

O sure, I said smiling.

Sure, he said, I know what it takes for winning. I'm a natural winner. It's got to be. I feel it in my bones. Look, I want to win. I'm strong. I feel good. It ain't natural I shouldn't be winning. I like to beat everybody. I like to beat everybody in the world.

I don't, I said.

I saw Ganz come in as Clara opened the locked door, peeking out first through the hole with a tin eye over it. I heard him say, Well they got Hoinck.

Belle screamed. All the glum people got up and started to get out the alley door. Run you rats, Belle shouted, and they had to make her stop shaking Ganz, and Ack was shouting, I told him not to take it on the lam. Ganz straightened his coat and tie and put out a cigarette on the floor which set Belle off. What do you think this is, she said, a barn? How come they got him? Is he taking the rap for you?

Ack kept spouting—I told him, There's a big election coming up. You'll be a patsy for the big guys. They have to show they're shutting up the speakeasies. You'll take the rap.

Shut up, Belle said starting to shake Ack, and Ganz said, Hoinck knows which side his bread is buttered. This ain't no funeral. He'll be out by morning. Lay low for a couple of days and everything will be the same as per usual. Give us a shot, Belle.

Belle said, Ganz, they took everything. Would those cops leave you a thimble?

You know damn well you got some put away, Ganz said.

To my surprise Belle went out with Clara and came back with a round of drinks.

Ack said, Those big guys they eat the little guys like us.

Belle said to me, The damn fool. He'll talk himself right out of house and home.

6

Customers kept knocking and nobody paid any attention. Finally Clara would open the door a little bit and say, Sorry you can't have nothin'. Hoinck just got knocked off. And the customers would beat it. There was a knock, two long, two short. Ganz got up and opened the door and a thin man came in. Ganz said this is my lawyer, Mr. Hone. Nobody said anything. He sat down at the table.

He said, Well you folks don't need to worry. I'll fix everything up in the morning. I guess he can stand it for one night.

Belle looked like she hated him. Her eyes were deep black with shadows under them and her mouth looked blue.

Hone said, Well maybe I'll get him out tonight. Look, I'm always on hand to help any of Ganz's boys. Don't worry about anything. Let me do the worrying.

I said, What I would like to know is who the stool is.

Hone drank his straight in one gulp and said he had to go down the street to see another guy who had been knocked off and for nobody to worry, everything would be all right in the morning and we would just have to lay low for a few days and it would be worth our while.

Ganz got up and they both went out and Ack jumped up and began walking the floor again. Take that job as a stool, he said to me. Go ahead. Everybody's a stool. If you aren't a stool you will be a stool. We're all stools. Get what I mean? Everybody stools on somebody else. Everybody's got to do it to live, see? You got to live. Don't you have to live? Yes or no? All right then you have got to be a stool sooner or later. Humanity, he says, flea-bitten humanity has got to live and they have got to stool.

For the Lord's sake and the Virgin Mary's shut your mouth, Belle cried.

I got to get out of this joint, it's getting me. Let's get out, she said to me. You guys got to scram, I'm going to lock up. The customers can pound on the door all night for all of me.

Everyone went out except Ack who still sat at the table and Belle put fifty cents on the table and told Ack to go out and get some apple pie for Hoinck's breakfast and be sure not to forget it.

Clara and Belle and I went out on the street. It was just nice and cool. Belle said, I've got a gallon but those guys are not going to get any of it. Hoinck will have to have some when he gets out. Maybe we'll throw a party.

I said, Aren't you going to sell anymore?

O, sure, she said. After a few days this will all die down.

Clara said, Why don't you explain it to the infant?

Belle laughed, She's too young.

I said, Well I would like to know why you are so sure he will get out in the morning. You were excited a little bit and then when that Hone came in you weren't excited anymore, and now you aren't worried.

Clara said, Listen, green, you want to know who the stool is, well Ganz is the stool.

They both laughed at my expression. They worked it like this, Belle said. Ganz is a big guy, he's got a lot of rackets. Hone is his lawyer, he's in on the take too. Ganz knows a lot of people. We couldn't keep bootlegging after hours if it wasn't for the protection Ganz gives us. Well, there's a big election coming up and the mayor's running again and he's got to do something to please the public, so there has got to be a clean-up so all of the so-called respectable people will vote for his party. So the mayor calls Ganz up to bat and tells him to let him choke out a few of his addresses, some little joints like ours, see, so as not to offend anybody. Then in the morning they will have something to print in the paper, see? So Hoinck is the fall guy this time, that's all.

We walked along the river. It smelled good. Belle said, Hoinck is scared of a gat, it makes him nervous. That's why Ganz plays along with Hoinck. He knows he won't go in for anything bigger or try to muscle in on their racket. Although Ganz has been promising Hoinck something big to set him up in a better racket.

I didn't know Hoinck was scared of anything, I said.

Belle said, I used to live with a guy in Chicago wasn't scared of a gat, and O, Christ, it was awful. Hoinck isn't such an angel. You know, when I had that black eye and said I hit it on the cupoard, well he did it the bastard, and then he says don't tell anybody. He don't want anybody to know he'd rob his own grandmother. The other night we was playing cards and Hoinck got mad and turned over the table and hit the other two guys in the jaw. I got so mad I put him out and then him and Ack stayed out all day Saturday and I had to take care of the customers. When he gets drunk and mad and he sees anybody he don't like he lets 'em have it. He's nuts, that's what he is, nuts and I don't see why I live with him, why I put up with him a minute on this earth.

But listen kid, she said, I'm telling you something. She looked at me and her face was wonderful. She said, Jesus Christ, Goddamn him I love him that's why I'm hooked like this all my life, Goddamn him I love him.

And a popcorn wagon was whistling down the street coming back from the parks. It was cool and we pulled our coats around us closer and I said, Let's get some popcorn.

The popcorn was puffy and good and it had a lot of salt and that stuff that tastes like butter.

That night after we got back, it must have been about four o'clock in the morning, a taxi drove up in front and Belle and I looked out the window and we saw Ack and Hoinck get out. We could just see the tops of their heads and Belle began to cry, There they are! Now they've come back for me to take care of. Now they'll be sick as dogs and they've come back for me to take care of.

We could see them look through all their pockets and then the taxi driver came upstairs and began pounding on the door. Ack and Hoinck were trying to get upstairs together, we could hear them scuffling in the hall and Belle turned out the light so they would hurt themselves.

The taxi driver said, Do you know these men?

Belle cried, Do I know them! I've been married to one of the lousy scum for over thirty years!

The taxi driver said, How do I know they belong here?

Belle said, You must be new to this town if this is the first time you've brought that merry couple here.

He said, I am, I just come from Chicago. How do I know I ain't leaving them in some gyp house?

Well, I didn't know the taxi men had joined a church, Belle said.

Ack and Hoinck loomed in the darkness, hanging on to each other. Belle went to Hoinck and put her arms around him and said to him, Honey don't you want to go to bed?

Sure, Hoinck said, I'll go to bed with you but who the hell are you?

The taxi driver said, You see this isn't your husband.

She said, Sure he's my husband. I'll prove it. If he doesn't do just like I say you can take him to jail.

O.K., he said.

O.K., she said, he'll come in there and he'll go through all his pockets and then he'll say, honey have you got any money? I owe this guy. If he doesn't do that you can take him to jail and I'll call for him in the morning.

O.K., the taxi man said, it's a go.

They all came in the room which we hadn't cleaned yet. Ack and Hoinck stood under the light and Hoinck started to go through all his pockets, first his pants pockets, front and back, and then all his coat pockets, and then his vest pockets, and then through his pants again, and coat and vest and pants again, and then he stood there a minute and then he said to Belle, Honey have you got any money? I owe this guy.

The taxi man nearly cracked his sides laughing. He said, You win. I guess you've been married to him all right.

Belle gave the taxi man a drink and paid him. Hoinck and Ack went to sleep the minute they hit the bed and you could hear their snores clean down the hall.

I slept on a couch because it was too late to go to my room.

I kept seeing Butch and Bill fading out of there, drinking too much for getting the job in the morning.

And in the night I thought I heard soldiers marching through the streets and I was sure I heard gunfire. And I heard Belle and Hoinck shouting and making love and crying all night.

7

It was sure Blue Monday. We didn't let in any customers. We could feel it was dangerous on the street. Some of the National Guard knocked on the door, almost banged it down, but Clara peeked out and saw the uniforms and put the extra bolt on the door. I thought I heard shooting far off. But Belle said, Nonsense, it was tires blowing out that was all. About noon Belle and Hoinck kind of crept out for more of the hair of the dog, as they called it. Clara and I cooked up some old hamburger. Nothing was left of the Booya.

It must have been about one o'clock when Butch's knock sent us all running. He came in the door quick and I saw his coat was torn and his arm was bloody.

Shut the door, he said, they're after me.

I got him to the booth and Belle ran for a basin of water.

Who's after you?

Don't talk.

Where's Bill? he suddenly shouted. He was running behind me. Look out and see if you see him.

Don't open the door, Belle said.

Butch seemed to kind of pass out. Belle said, He's just been beaten. He ain't been shot.

There was another knock at the door, three long and two short, which meant a customer. Clara looked out then opened the door and old Josh was holding Bill up as if he was walking but his head hung down. Clara and Belle got under his arms and they sat him on a chair but he fell over and when they straightened him up you could see a huge red circle on his shirt.

He's almost dead. He's been shot, Belle cried.

For a long time Butch held his head. I noticed Butch's hand on the black head of his brother and Bill had one hand resting on his knee like he was just sitting there waiting, except his face got whiter and the blood seemed to be coming out of both ears.

It was a scab job, Butch said, they locked us in the plant. They sent me out to fix a light on the loading platform. I was fixing a big bulb and they came to get me and I dropped a live wire in the middle of them and they beat me up.

Who?

The strikers, you dope, the men who worked there. The men I was scabbing on.

Clara called the police. They came pretty quick and said Bill was dead. I knew that already a few minutes before they got there. They carried the chair into the kitchen and threw a tablecloth over him and he still sat upright in the chair. A cop said, We'll send for the morgue wagon and Butch stood in front of his brother. O, no, he said, he ain't going to no morgue. He's my brother.

The cop said, O.K., kid so he's your brother, so what?

Butch looked like he was going to hit him but he didn't. He said to Belle who was crying in a loud voice, Call Peck and Nordstrom, they're the best undertakers in town.

Belle said, Listen, honey you better call Swinson, that's a cheaper place and just as good work besides he's an old friend of mine and he'll—

Shut up, Butch yelled at her and his neck swelled like snakes.

Belle said, I'll get Ganz, he can get a discount.

But Ganz was gone.

We left Butch in the kitchen and we could see him through the service window standing by the figure under the white tablecloth.

The cops kept coming in and drinking our beer free while Clara spent all afternoon typing out a sign with one finger which said, "Tonight is Turkey Night!" They kept looking at the blood in the kitchen where the chair sat. About all they seemed to be sure of was that Bill was dead and we knew that already.

Butch kept saying over and over, No sir, officer, my brother never had an enemy in the world. Nobody would be the enemy of my brother, everybody will tell you that. My brother was a self-respecting citizen. He would have got up in the world. Nobody can tell you different.

Aw, nuts! the cops said.

We took in fifteen dollars before three o'clock just at horses and that's good even for Saturday, much less Monday.

After Butch got through talking to the cops he would come in the kitchen where I was washing dishes and he would look like he just licked up some cream. I'm telling them, baby, he would say. These lousy cops ain't going to tell me what to do. Looka this, baby.

He showed me a picture in the paper of Bill as a baby and of their mother standing by a vine, smiling.

He's my brother, he almost shouted. Now I know what I got to do. Now I know it.

I didn't know what he meant. Clara was excited and scared. I was scared too but it was exciting. About four we sat in the kitchen and had a cup of coffee and Clara got to be telling me about death. She told me that she was going to commit suicide once, so she was very familiar with death. She said she left home, stayed away for a long time till she was afraid to go back. She said she was living in a room with a sailor. She said she got tired of it after three days. It wasn't much, she said, not like it is in the movies. She would have gone home but she was afraid. She said she went every day to the river to commit suicide. She wrote her mother a long letter about it which began, Dearest Mother, when you get this I will be dead, dead do you understand! She said sailors and soldiers were easy to pick up and sometimes you had fun but three days was a lot of it. She said she met her mother on the streetcar one day and went home with her because she didn't care what happened to her.

But she said that always made her know death real well. She said the only reason she was alive now and not dead like Bill, the only thing that kept her from it was on account of something interesting would be happening just as she was about to do it. Like once a swell soldier came across the bridge and asked her to have a beer with him, and you always want to do what you can for a soldier, it's only patriotic. Another time she forgot what she was going to do on account of it was such a sweet day and the leaves were just coming out and there was some kids and some ducks on the river having fun.

Finally the undertaker Butch called came and they took Bill out in a basket and Butch went along and all I could do was run out and give him his cap and he took it.

8

Next day I tried to wait on Butch, get him stuff all day long, and he would look at me and pat my arm. Finally he said, Don't you want to go and see him?

Who? I said like an idiot.

Why, Bill, he said. They fixed him up nice. He looks real lifelike. Gee, he looks good. Come on.

No, I don't want to do it.

Why, he looks just like he always looks. It's the best job there is. I got the best for my brother. They fixed him up good. I want you to see it, the way they do it. It costs a lot of money, but hell! I want to do it up brown.

On the way, Butch kept talking about his brother. I listened to every word he said. He said Bill was an A1 ballplayer and, Gee, he was a sweet kid when he was young, smart as a whip.

We stopped in front of a swell building and Butch helped me out and we went up the stairs and a nurse met us and Butch said he wanted to see his brother. Who? she said. Bill Hinckley, Butch shouted. Oh, this way, she said and took us into an elegant room and before we knew it we were looking down at a wax face with paint on it, and the hair looked so black. It didn't look like Bill. It looked more like him when he was sitting under the sheet in the kitchen.

Butch seemed to like it. He whispered to me, They make over the face. He seemed to think it was something wonderful.

Those damn cops, he said, kept him so long investigating, rigor mortis, that's what they call it, set in, and they had to break his jaw.

Break his jaw? I whispered.

Sure. It looks O.K. It looks all right doesn't it? They do wonderful things nowadays. It's marvelous. It's wonderful.

I didn't think it was very wonderful.

Let's go, I said.

Scaredy, he said, and put his hand on my arm. I did get warm.

Yes, I said. I looked at him and saw how they both looked alike with those lean narrow heads, and that sharp nose like on a scent, and the high bones. I was afraid and I started to go out and he followed and we got in the car and began to drive fast to the country and it was early autumn.

I put my hand down on the seat between us to keep from falling on his side and he put his hand over mine.

Gee, he said, death is funny.

Yes, I said.

We went by the shanties on the levee.

You know, he said, I had a dream about death last week. Now there is something funny. I had dreamed it was like Bill was very pale and he was talking to me. Yes sir, that's pretty funny when you come to think of it.

I said, That's funny all right.

Just think, last week this time Bill and I was playing a game of pool.

Now he's gone. It's pretty funny when you come to think of it.

It's funny all right.

I didn't say anything. I didn't feel good.

Gee, you're cute. You got cute hands.

They were blistered from so much lye in the dishwater. I tried to take them away from him and hide them.

We came to a field and Butch stopped and for some reason I jumped out and ran across the road and looked back and called him, I don't know why I did it, and he jumped out of the car and ran after me and grabbed my arm from behind. I was scared. I didn't know why I did it.

He was trying to kiss me and he had hold of my arms tight, screwing them around. I got away and ran some more. We were in a pasture with short grasses. He came up and I said, Don't, Butch.

Why did you get out and run?

I don't know, I said, I didn't mean to.

You egged me on, he said, you got me going, now it's your fault. You got to take the consequences.

I was surprised.

You got to take your medicine, he said, you egged me on. You did it on purpose. You got me all riled up now. You can't say I wasn't treating you like a sister and then you jumps out of the car and runs like a harlot.

I didn't, I said, I didn't mean anything.

She didn't mean anything! he said to the sky. Godalmighty, here I been hot as a hound for a week and trying to act nice to you because you are such a nice girl and then all of a sudden you egg me on.

Clara was right. I didn't understand men. I felt very sad.

I'm sorry, I said, if I hurt you so much.

Good Christ! he says, what we got to take from women! You don't know what a man suffers.

I guess I don't, I said.

We walked slow back to the car.

That's the way it is, he said, nobody appreciates how good you are. Everybody tries to get it on you. I want to beat everybody down. I want victory, that's what I want. I want to beat everyone in the world. I want to rob people of faith and then not give them anything.

O no, I cried.

Yes, that's it, that's what I want to do all right. Don't tell me what to do. I been batting from hell to breakfast and now I'm going to do something. I got to be better than anybody. Don't put on airs. You like to beat too.

No, I don't.

Sure, you do. What do you like to do then?

O, I don't know, I said, I like to be. I like to feel good that's what I like.

There it goes again, he said, there it is. Women are dunces. They never say anything definite. O Godchrist, women! Women'll ruin your life quicker than scat.

I wanted to give him something. I looked at the sky and the grass. I thought maybe there was some quail in the grass. We walked back and I felt he didn't like me now. He would never like me.

It was getting darker and he said after we got in the car, Gee, I'm lonely, and without looking at me at all he took my hand.

Maybe he did like me a little then.

He said, Gee, love me a little kid.

I said, O Butch, I don't know how.

Gee, you're a little sweet kid, he said, you're so little, and he looked at me hungry.

I thought, if you slept with a man could you turn out the light before so he wouldn't see how how thin you were?

How about it? he said. Don't you want to? We're both lonely and you're scared.

He looked scared too but I didn't tell him that. I couldn't move. He kissed me then opening my mouth a little.

Jesus, he said.

I was scared. Maybe he didn't like it. Maybe I hadn't done it right.

Jesus, he said, I don't believe you ever did kiss a guy before, like you said.

No, I said.

Honest? he said.

Sure.

Jesus!

We drove past the stockyards and stopped to have a cup of coffee and doughnuts and when I swallowed I could taste for him, and I was trying to think how it would feel to be him.

When he had eaten three doughnuts I jumped up with the plate and got him two more and held them under his drooping head.

O mama, what can I do?

O mama, you told me it would be dangerous.

O mama, I'm scared . . . what did you do?

9

When I got the letter from papa I was surprised. It made me kind of sick. When he writes a letter it is because he wants to blame you for something. He wants to make something clear. He always thought we all betrayed him some way. He only had to look at me to want to hit me good and plenty. I thought it was because he saw that wanting in me. I too wanted something very bad just like he wanted it.

The last move we made after trading the farm that had only plums and honey—what did we know about farming?—We moved back to the old house and I'll never forget that house. When I left it to come to St. Paul mama was standing by the window crying, in that old wooden house with the doors hanging on the hinges, and the windows slanting and the shutters screeching in the wind. Mama's white face in the dim of the window as if she would never see me again. The last thing she said—Don't tell anyone about Marilyn, what the Lord has brought upon us, and now you going to Sodom. Marilyn was lost in a dope ring they said. I didn't even turn to wave to her, or open my mouth or howl or say a word.

It seems like my family was crippled and hurt just as much as if their flesh had been riddled by bullets and their limbs torn apart. Them losing their children one way or another. The last son walking down the road and never saying a living word again. And the beauty Marilyn, prettier than me, pride of his eye being ground in the manure of the city. I left because papa was driven to a fury sitting down with all the mouths to feed. We had to eat in relays. He had a dark and stormy love for his children and the only thing he could be sure of for them was disaster.

So I knew when I got the letter from him it was something terrible and I didn't want to open it.

Butch said, I'll open it for you. Fathers should be lost at sea, buried in the wild West, send a postal card from Canada or Alaska. What the hell. So he opened the letter and started to laugh and read, Ingot Iron Shop, Quality Work with Quality Iron. To my datter . . . I tore the letter away from him and held it to me.

You never forget your father, I said, he is like dead eye sockets looking at you.

It seems like my father was born to fail, I said, he was mixed up in more kind of failing than you can shake a stick at.

He was just no good, Butch said.

No he was good. Something was against him, all his working didn't make no difference. He worked, he tried, he was always looking for something better, always trading something thinking he was going to fall into something great, something that would end all our troubles tomorrow.

It was when I was three years old I remember my mother praying all night that he would come to his senses but he came back from a trip he was on and said he had traded the nice city house for a farm in Wisconsin, a bee and plum farm. What do you know about bees and plums? my mother cried. Nothing, my father

26

said, but think of it, honey and plums, that will be different from the coal mines where I was raised. It sounded like the Bible. Mama wept all night.

We went to this farm. The bees were in the valley and the hills behind. It was nice. We had two cows. One cow licked my brother in the ear so he couldn't hear. My mother said it was a judgment. My mama sat all summer making a lace dress so she wouldn't remember that my sister was not bright. Jim started to raise some rabbits and when he asked how long the buck should be left with the doe everybody howled and nobody knew how long. Just when we had a nice bunch of rabbits they all died overnight with disease.

The potatoes got hard in the ground that year. The kids dug them up and put them in a pile and the cow and horse got loose and ate them and swelled up. They punctured the belly of the cow with the butcher knife and she went down but the horse choked to death and died.

During the drought everything was dying then and mama cried all day thinking her children would be next, saying what had the Lord against papa now when he had worked all his life, been righteous, done his best, worked his fingers to the bone.

I remember when I first went out to work when my mother's seventh son was born. I was eleven then. The welfare sent me out to work for Mrs. Cranack for my room and board and my mother said one less mouth to feed. My father didn't say anything. He just looked leaner and sadder and gave me a quarter and looked like he was going to say something but he didn't.

And when I came back from Mrs. Cranack's because the old man was coming into my room every night, wanting to get in bed with me, my father didn't say a thing. He just kept on smoking when I came in and patted me on the back as I passed him in the kitchen. When he asked me how they treated me and I told him I worked eighteen hours a day there he just looked at me and kept on smoking.

I remember all the houses where we were living, the old halls, the rooms where Joe the brother just before me was born. My mother always had her babies easy. My father was proud of that. Look at that, he would say, some old lady, just has them on the floor and then gets up and gets supper.

Let the dead bury the dead, Butch said, you never asked to be born. It was their kicks getting you, wasn't it? Nobody held a pistol to their head. Are you gonna read the letter or ain't you? I tell you my papa was a card. A good gambling man. Just came back to lay my mama and have another brat. Then he'd horse off to another scene. They say he was a handsome devil. Well, look at me.

Do you want to hear the letter from my papa?

Well sure, I don't care. My papa sent a card now and then with a mountain scene on it, saying I am fine how are the kiddies. Wish you were here. But it never said where he was. Some old man. . . .

Shall I read the letter from my papa? I thought I wouldn't be so scared if Butch was to hear it. I knew I'd be awful scared when I finished it alone. I thought it meant he wasn't going to live long.

I could see his terrible eyes. I couldn't tell if it was worse out loud or if I read it to myself.

27

Dear Datter, it began. He never went beyond sixth grade. He could yell that at you like a terrible oath.

The letter said:

Ingot Iron Shop.
Quality work
with quality
iron.

Art Schaffer. Sheet Metal and
Furnace reparing.

To my datter; I received your letter and I am reely suprised how come you wrote to me are you reely anxious to know if I am steel alive?

And did you change your mind about that good for nothing father of yours?

Well if it is the first thing I am telling you that I am steel existing not living. I have no job to speeck of and no shop eether. Just doing an od job when I get one. financially I am ruined. Fisicaly I am a broken men and mentally lord knows if your mother and all the rest that are the cause of my present condition are satisfied what they have done to me.

Then let them enjoy themselves.

There will be a day even if I will not live to see it but a day will come and they will all gett their punishment and if you say again that all of this is self pitty then you do not need to write any more to me.

The best years of my life I have sacrificed for all of you and now that I am left in this condition I want to be alone with my missery.

All the love that I did have in my heart for all my Children has been burned out and only a sore spot is left.

I have ansered your letter to satisfy you curiostiy.

Whatever got in your mind to write to me your no good father.

You're not able to do to me any more harm than what you have already done to me.

My conscience is clear and clean. Lord knows I have done my duty to my children and if you think different then the pleasure is yours.

Goodbye and good luch and may my grandchildren punish my children the same as they have punished me.

your father,
Art Schaffer.

Butch had fallen asleep.

I put the letter in my pocket.

My father's terrible face seemed to be asleep like Butch's. His eyes closed forever over the terrible accusing.

I *wished* he could die.

10

My hunch was right about papa. The next week I got a letter special delivery saying he was dead. Mama said to come. I was glad to get away awhile. Butch was after me night and day. I loved him but I was afraid of that. I didn't know what to do. We were near crazy with it.

My folks lived up the river in a village. It only takes two hours.

I saw the old house as the bus went through. I knocked at the door. My mother came. She looked smaller than ever and older. O, Girl, she cried, they'll blame me. You don't think they'll blame me?

What for? I said. She smelled funny.

It wasn't my fault, she said. Why should they blame me? A doctor costs a lot.

Didn't you call the doctor, mama?

She threw her apron over her head. You see, they'll blame me. O, we couldn't afford it Girl, the expense. It's lucky he died so quick without no illness. I always say it's the best way to do.

It was the same old wooden house, the same cold rooms crowded with my mother's seven children, still home, even though Joe is twenty-two, older than me. We went past the front room. I knew why. We went into the dining room and all the kids said hello. My mother was still crying and whining. I couldn't look at her.

Besides, it isn't my fault, she cried looking at me with one eye over her apron. I told Fred—he's the man next door who was over here—I told him, and now I wish I hadn't I should've known if you want anything done do it yourself, I told him to telephone and I thought he would straight away. I am never going to tell anyone, have anyone do anything ever again. Your father would never blame me.

Her eye kept looking at me. What happens to women? What awful things do they know?

Would you like to see him? Joe said. Joe is a mechanic but he hasn't got a job. He's about the same age as Butch. He put his hand on mama's shoulder. I could never do that. I could never touch mama. Joe said that it was a good thing it wasn't summer now.

Why? I said.

Because papa would begin to smell.

To smell? I said.

Sure, he said, the county's supposed to get him and they haven't come, he's been there two days now and he's still got his own juice in him.

For Lord's sake, I said.

I told them relief people to come right away, I let them know, mama said, that's the way they do it. We ain't got no coal, we ain't got hardly no food, just a little rice. Now if we had a ham hock . . .

Alie the six year old said, Do we want a wreath for papa? Papa ought to have some flowers.

Mama said, Come and see him. What could we have on it? We can't afford a wreath girl, what are you talking about? But if we could would we have HUSBAND or FATHER in carnations? O, carnations is a lovely flower.

I always called him nothing but Mr. Schaffer, mama giggled a little still looking at me with one eye. We never called him father, always pa.

Or papa, the kids pipe up. You can't put pa on a wreath.

It's his funeral, Joe said. When you're dead you're dead and you ain't hungry no more.

We went in. He was lying on the couch and mama had lit some ends of candles. There was my father. I looked at his face. The big walrus mustache looked alive and funny. His eyes were shut. I was glad he couldn't see me to roar at me. He would never roar at me again or strike me. His black eyebrows flew up fierce and active like mice feeding on his face.

The last time I saw him he was walking around yelling about how many mouths he had to feed, with a grey beard on his cheeks and his grey underclothes hanging loose from sleeping in them. He was mad because mama wanted to go on relief. I worked all my life, he was shouting, and as long as I got two hands at the ends of my arms I'm gonna feed my own family, ain't any lady reliefers gonna snoop around here I tell you, you hear me?

Mama came up close and looked around at me with her small frightened face as if apologizing for everything. When I saw mama's face I wanted to cry. Not before. It's like we never knew him. What is father? She never knew him. He beat her, gave her children.

O, he was a good man, mama said, he was a good man, he was a good provider. If there was anything to do he would find it.

Aw nuts, Joe said, he was a lunkhead.

Shut up, I said. O mama . . .

Mama said, O Girl, and her face puckered and she began to cry without making a noise, as if she didn't want to bother anybody with it.

The younger girls put some coffee on the table. It did seem like there was an odor around the house. It made me sick. I didn't say anything.

Mama kept talking in a low voice, rolling her eyes at the door, as if papa still might be coming in to shout at us.

She started telling me all about the children. I could look up and see their frightened eyes in the room, listening to everything she said.

We always been poor, mama said, had a hard time to get along but we never lived so bad as now. I ain't so good in health now either, I am broken in health.

Angel is a fine girl, she said. Good to her parents. Stasia is different. She is very mean lately and doesn't answer when her papa speaks and slams the doors behind her. She was bad to her papa. He made her leave school to look for work. We had to have money, Girl. She was mad and worked in a factory for two days only and we had to take the money. She began to be so ugly to her father that he would not speak to her and once he got so excited he fainted. Stasia is very neat and clean and loves to bathe herself often but she should not talk like that to her papa. Is it his fault he cannot get a job or bring home anything? It was papa's position that children owe their parents something.

Aw nuts, Joe said.

Sh . . . I said. Go on, mama.

My sons are good, mama said. Henry is nervous but not a bad boy. Papa always wanted his boys to do the right thing. When you were all little, she said, we had less trouble. But Stasia, O Stasia was bad to her papa. She would come and see him sitting at the table and she couldn't look at him.

Stasia stood up. He wanted to be king, to boss, she said. Because he was a failure he wanted others to be so that they wouldn't be better than him. When he read the paper out loud we couldn't say a word, he said we should not talk but listen. . . .

Helen said, But if papa tried to whip you, you would go dancing around waving your arms and this made him mad. You should let him whip you.

Stasia began to cry. He beat me before people. Now he'll never beat me again. I'm glad he's dead.

Nobody said anything.

Mama said, I think the home needs love.

Nobody said anything.

Now I'll live only for you children, she said, I hope you will get on better. I hope you will get more education. I hope you won't have it like papa and me.

Nobody said anything. Then Helen said, Thank you mama.

How did papa die? I said. He was all right last week and now he is dead.

They all looked at each other.

Joe said, I asked papa if I could take his tools.

Mama said quick, Those tools were all papa had left, he loved them, he had them a long time.

Well, I wasn't going to hurt them none, I had a chance to pick up a little money and he told me not to take them and I took them anyway.

Stasia said, Then he got up and began tearing around the house like mad and mama said you better watch for Joe and warn him and I sat at the window all evening but I fell asleep, and Joe came in the back way so I didn't see him.

Joe said, Papa waited in the dark and when I came in the room and got my clothes off so I was naked as a jay then he jumped out and grabbed me and beat me with a strap.

Everybody looked down.

If he whipped me in broad daylight open and aboveboard, Joe said, I wouldn't mind, but he pounded on me in the dark and he said I was with a girl and jumped on me like an animal in the dark.

Henry said, I come down and mama held the hand of papa and said don't strike my son and we were all at the bottom of the stairs looking at

31

him and he began to roar down at us, You're all against me, the hand of every man is against me, and he began to moan and cry.

Joe said, He let me go and began to cry like a whipped dog. It was awful. It scared us worse than his yelling.

I'll go away, he kept shouting, I'll go away. Get me a pillow slip I'll put my earthly belongings in, I'll go away, that's what I'll do. I worked like a slave all my life. I worked, I grubbed, I did everything a father could do. I worked day and night for my children he said, I built houses for my children. I walked this country looking for work, looking asking here there everywhere for work. . . .

We all looked at each other.

Gee, it was awful, Joe said.

He did too, mama said. You children don't what it is to have eleven mouths to feed day in and day out.

Well, whose fault is it? Joe said. Did we ask to be born?

Sh . . . sh . . . mama said.

Stasia said, Then mama wouldn't sleep with him and she came into bed with me and he came in and said that a woman's place was beside her husband and then he swore a bloody streak and went out with his clothes in the pillow slip and mama cried all night saying, I'll leave him after forty years, you'll see I'll leave him one of these days and then what will become of him? What will happen to him? O, I'll never marry as long as I live. I hate men. I'll never, never marry.

He was a good father, mama said.

The funniest part was, Joe said, that he slept right out under the apple tree not ten feet from the house. . . .

All the kids began to giggle.

The next morning, mama said, your poor father came in white as a ghost. Sleeping in the damp brought on his dock trouble.

I'll never marry a man, Stasia said. . . .

Haw, Joe said, listen to her.

I won't. How could you do it, mama? Papa just going around giving you kids.

He was my husband, mama said.

I wouldn't have nothing to do with it, Stasia said.

Remember when papa always read the want ads? Joe said. Papa was a swapper.

O, a swapper from way back, Henry cried.

Remember the time we went out to see a house and land and the land was under water?

We all looked at each other and Stasia laid her head on the table, her shoulders shaking.

Papa was the berries. Here is something good, papa would say, and he would read the ad out like if there was something thrown in all the better.

O, papa was looking for something thrown in all right.

Children! mama cried. Her face was puckered and she let out little gasps. I put my arm around her laughing. Remember papa was going to trade Henry once for a tire.

O, my! mama cried, her eyes startled. O, my!

O, Christ! Joe laughed, leaning against the door.

Henry shouted and jumped up and down, catching his own shins in his hands.

O, my! mama cried, it was only for a few hours while we went to town. . . . Your papa. . . .

O, Christ! Joe shouted, his mouth open laughing. He would trade off the Virgin Mary.

She wouldn't be no good to him, Joe howled.

Remember the house he built on a rock and in a storm it would rock back and forth and we couldn't say a word. . . .

It never fell down, mama cried, it never did fall down.

No, it didn't, Henry said, it didn't but we fell out of it sometimes. . . . O, papa!

Everybody was laughing and we were happy. There was a way to laugh because papa was dead. It seemed funny but it seemed all right.

Now you're single, mama, Joe said, you can have a good time, dance and go around and drink beer like the merry widows. . . .

Joe, mama cried, ain't you ashamed, and your father not cold yet. . . .

O, he's cold. Phew . . . he's dead all right.

Stop it, mama cried, O stop. She threw her apron over her head.

Mama! mama! Joe said, picking her up in his arms and swinging her above us all.

Land sakes, mama cried.

Mama, if I was a millionaire I'd take you on a spree, I'd buy you some candy and crackerjacks, I don't care if we never get back.

O! O! she cried, hanging onto his strong neck for dear life.

We had supper of rice.

They say the poor in China have to eat through a wall of rice, Joe said, I think we about did our wall. . . .

We're lucky to have rice, mama said.

I couldn't go to bed. After I washed the dishes I started to scrub the floor. I began scrubbing everything. I scrubbed the kitchen and the entry. I remembered how once papa was leaning on a broom and I thought, O, papa I would like to kiss you. I didn't do it because I was scared. I thought that I could pretend I had fallen asleep or tripped and caught him around the neck but I didn't do it.

I went in after everyone was asleep but Joe was sitting in the room smoking a pipe.

He smiled at me. Kill the smell, he said.

It was quiet. I didn't look at papa's face. But I scrubbed the floor clean all around him.

11

Joe went downtown. I heard mama coming downstairs and I thought, How light she's getting. I could hardly hear her step, so timid like a frightened animal.

O mama, I called, and she came into the room.

Girl, she said, what are you doing up this late? You should get your rest. What have you been doing? Scrubbing, O, she said ashamed, I haven't scrubbed lately, you must think the house is awful dirty, but you see how it is I was saying yesterday to Stasia, we must scrub. I am sorry, Girl, that the house is so dirty. . . .

No mama, the house is clean, I said, I just wanted to do something. I'm used to carrying beer all day. I need exercise.

O, she said, do you have to work in that awful place? I brought you up decent and good and now you have to work in a bad immoral place like that. Your father didn't like it. He didn't like going on relief, either. He said he never asked a cent of charity in his whole life and he died like he was born, not owing a cent. No sir, we don't owe a cent.

My mother seemed proud of my father. I looked at her. I wanted to ask her a million questions. I wanted to tell her about Butch. About having to decide something.

Mama, I said, were you ever sorry you married papa?

Land sakes, mama said, O my heavens to Betsy. . . . Sorry for marrying your father! What would become of me if I hadn't? Forty years I lived with your father, had his children. Land sakes, child, what's got into you, asking such a heathenish question of your mama?

We sat down. Papa looked like he was just asleep on the couch. Only he was whiter and thinner like some awful thunder had gone out of him.

Mama sat very straight like a young girl. After all that's happened to her. Outside you could hear children, and then you didn't hear them anymore playing anteover, then it was quiet with just the sounds of birds sometimes.

O it's too bad, mama said, it's too bad, papa should have a nice casket. I remember for my father we had a nice casket, grey with wreaths around in carnations saying FATHER, HUSBAND.

Those words hurt me, father, husband.

Mama went on talking. Go on mama, I said, talk, it will do you good. Go on, talk.

Maybe she would tell me something. Maybe out of all the words something would come through and I would see what to do. Whatever you say, mama had something, she had her life, her children, she knows what it is even if she can't say it right out. She knows something. She knows what it's about. She has felt something.

The times we had, mama said, child, Girl, he looks now like he did on his wedding day. O, we had a wedding day though, an elegant wedding, she said, and everybody paying to dance and a whole boilerful of wine made from plums. He got two dollars a day then, only ten hours work and two dollars. But every night I felt him lighter and barking like a wolf. Your papa never had it nice. I wanted something nice for him but he never had it. Once I surprised him. I remember how surprised I was. Why Emily, he says to me. He was surprised.

What did you do, mama?

I tell you it was in the depression, some depression we had way back. This ain't the first depression. I disremember what year it was. But it was bad. People were starving. We lost our house, your papa couldn't get a thing, men were standing in breadlines a block long, it's a fact. My, it was bad and when you're hungry, and you got all those mouths to feed, you get busy as a mouse covering a mountain. Well sir, I surprised him, didn't I Mr. Schaffer, I surprised you good.

What did you do, mama?

Well sir, I got me some rags, I picked up old overalls men threw away on the dock and I washed them clean as all get out, and split them up and I wove a rug and I took it to the butcher on the sand bar and he traded with me for a whole sheep. It was as good a rug as ever you'd want, and well sir, he gave me a whole sheep for it. The boys carted it home and hung it in the coal shed, it was winter I remember, and when you came home from school I said, Look Girl I got a whole sheep. A whole sheep? you said.

That was me?

Yes Girl, that was you and a cute tyke you were. . . .

Go on mama.

Mama, where? you said. I put my hand on my mouth to keep from smiling. Look, See! I put my apron around you from the wind and opened the shed door and there it hung straight from its two feet tied together and the place bleeding where I had cut out a piece for stew. O, the beautiful sheep, I remember them from the old country. There he was, hanging there, and I got him to feed my husband and the lean crying stomachs of my children that you could never be filling. . . .

O mama, you must have had it hard.

Pshaw, child, that was nothing. Your father and I had it good.

She looked at him.

I can remember the smell of that mutton to this very day, she said, the good odor of meat plucking right at your marrow when you haven't eaten it for a spell.

Mama was hungry now.

Everyone had to see it when they came in, smiling and looking, shouting, Mutton! real mutton! mama, where did you get it? They all looked up to me that day. I had to laugh. I felt like laughing and singing. All my children coming with their nipped faces taking a smell of the warm mutton smell and they all got dressed up and washed without no telling them. I tell you that was something. We looked out the window for your papa and the men who had work were going by with their pails. I tell you evening is a bad time for women looking for men to come home and your papa coughing like that so I rubbed his chest and his hard dock muscles, O, he was a sight to see then, he was a strong man, a sight to see, a sight for sore eyes. Every single night I would lie there and he would cough and spit up blood. And then there he was with everybody yelling and all that much children in a shack can make a powerful heap of noise, you get used to it so it seems awful quiet without papa. It's going to be awful quiet. Papa's coming, they was yelling, papa's coming, and there he was in the door looking at us kind of angry like he always was. I always said that the soot of the coal mines never got out of him. He was like the wrath of God, something strong and good in your papa. He was good to me.

Was he, mama?

Yes, never a man was better. He was good to me.

What is a man when he is good to you?

Mama looked at me. She began to pick at her apron. She smiled. Well, you're too young to know, she said, you're too young. But it's a good thing, a good man is a good thing.

Go on mama, what happened? Tell me.

I remember like it was yesterday. I was stirring the stew and smiling and kind of embarrassed because it was his job to get the meat and maybe he would be mad with me. He stood looking over my shoulder at the stew. He patted me on the back. All the kids was still as mice. I could feel all the eyes in the room, all my warm good-smelling children, their warm breath steaming the windows. He was standing there sharp as a hatchet and warm as a dove. He was a gentle man, but he was worried and bitten.

Emily, he said, and when he spoke like that to me it put a darkness over me. O sure I'll always see his lean face stretched over me, I'll always see it.

Don't cry, mama.

Emily! he said, how did you get it? Then they all began to shout, Mutton stew and fruit soup! A sheep! he said, when they told him, a whole sheep! O, he admired me then like he did when I had my children, he used to say nobody has children like Emily, listen to her yell, that's a yell for you, and she'll get up and get us our supper. O he admired me then. How did you do it? he said, and little smiles came out all over my flesh. Your papa could make me feel good when he wanted but life got hard and bitter for him, biting at his heels like a hound dog.

My little mama! he said, did you steal it? I laughed. Don't, I said, the children will see us, I didn't like you children to see us kissing.

Why, mama?

It comes soon enough. The children were quiet watching us and he said, Did you steal it, mama? I said I want you to have something nice. I stroked his head, I want you to have something nice. It's a fierce feeling you have for your husbnd and children like you could feed them your body, and chop yourself up into little pieces. The stew boiled over, sizzled, so then to dish it up. Ah, what a meal, what a meal, eyes looking at every move, careful one will get more, the precious meat. O I tell you, meat can be very precious and your mouth waters for it. There I saw all my children. I hope you'll marry a man like papa and have children, Girl. And papa said, Pitch to, and everybody started eating.

How old was I, mama?

You were ten if I remember. O it's good to live. You don't have to have much Girl, not much, we never asked for much. To know each other, touch, sing, feel it in your breast and throat. You have to live it and die it and then you know it. Nobody can tell you anything, Girl. You have to live it and sometimes you have to die it and then it's in you and you always know it.

He's a long man, not bent over now. When I bathed him and laid him out there I saw his muscles slack like old ropes on his strong bone. He wasn't made for the way they used him, that's a fact. He was made for different things. When he was a young man he had vinegar in him. Was it wicked, Girl? I looked at him naked, when I laid him out. I made all the children leave and looked at him a long time. Was it wicked? Was it a sin?

No mama.

I combed his mustache, it does look nice. It used to be hard to get the coal dust out. O, he was a pretty man, he was a well-made man, knit together. They used him bad. They made a bad wind in him. He made me good children, he made good children.

We sat there.

I said, You can marry again, mama, maybe.

She looked at me and I knew she never would. I couldn't understand. I always thought papa was a failure and mean.

The next day they came and got papa and took him away in a basket and carried him out easy, he had lost his weight. And mama stood in the middle of the room her apron over her head.

I didn't wait because the relief doesn't give any funeral. You just go to the cemetery where they have free burial. Mama felt bad about not having any wreaths for him and Helen and Ruth spent all morning covering walnuts with all the silver paper they had saved to sell for the Red Cross. Joe said he didn't see why it wasn't good as flowers but mama never heard of walnuts on a coffin and besides the relief wouldn't let them do it. I told them to go afterwards and they could make a little design of walnuts on the grave and papa would like that.

I had to leave. I had to get back anyway. Mama wanted to give me something. I told her I needed a blanket. I was ashamed to take it, but she made me.

Mama acted kind of crazy. She said I must better myself, get up in the world.

I hadn't told her about Butch.

I gave her three dollars, all I had, which was my rent, and she said I would come to a bad end, she could tell it and it was all because of those who preyed on young girls and I had to watch out in the city and not let any man get at me and remember what she had told me, and trust to our Lord who art in heaven.

All right, mama, I said.

She said she would come down there and make me lose that terrible job I had, in dens of iniquity, and I would come to an end like my sister, disappear in a dope ring like that, and never be heard of again, and I shouldn't work in a terrible beer joint like that, I should get something better, I should get up in the world, meet some nice men.

All right, mama.

And if anything happened to me, she said, her best child, in that bad city, in those dens of iniquity, she would jump off the bridge and kill herself, or we would find her some morning dead in her bed, dead of grief.

Goodbye, mama, goodbye.

12

I came back to the German Village a different person. Yes, I was different now, with my papa dead and gone and mama telling me everything. I was into my mama's life for the first time, and knew how she all the time, chased like by a pack of wolves, kept us alive, fierce and terrible. No matter what happened she put food into our mouths and there was something good about all that happened as if she had a secret. Mama had a secret. She let me feel it, let me know it. I wouldn't say I wasn't still afraid, hot and cold, like on a brink, but I knew I had to jump, be in it like mama.

I had given my last three bucks to mama. Belle and Hoinck had no money of course, Ganz was pushing them, and I even yelled at them, You pay me. Belle said, With what? Belle said it was only Ganz that was keeping them from being thrown out on their ear. They wouldn't tell me where Butch was and I couldn't wait on the customers there. I had to find him. No one seemed to have seen hide nor hair of him and I even felt that he was hiding in the backrooms, under the bars, down by the river hiding from me.

Clara says, If I was a john I'd hide from you. You look mighty beautiful and out to get it.

Get what? I cried, what am I going to get?

Clara laughed, Love O love O careless love. Watch out you don't wear your apron high and they'll pass your door. The best way to get the horse back in the barn is to get some good fresh hay. Don't look so bad, baby. Butch is nuts about you. He's scared he's caught.

It's me that's scared, I cried.

You come and stay with me, Clara said. I make enough off the johns to pay the rent and something over. You could make it good kid, it ain't nothing if you are always looking for something better. And you meet nice men too, that'll give you lace tablecloths and peasant pottery.

O, I cried, Clara I am getting ready to live, to know someone, to touch someone. Clara hugged me—It don't seem right to me, an angel like you kid it ain't right.

I got to find him, I said.

Just sit in the park, Clara said, and wait. He'll sniff you out like a hound dog.

I did sit in the park and every beer joint and bistro on Third. Have you seen Butch? I'd ask, and it got to be a joke, No we ain't seen Butch for a coon's age.

I had this feeling you have to hurry, like running in the woods with hunters after you and arrows going by you and into you. Then some days I thought I would never see him again. He had gone on the road, taken a freight, taken a powder, Clara said, gone gone.

I didn't see Ganz either, maybe they were holed up somewhere.

I didn't want to sleep, I dreamed about it every night. It was Butch in the grave instead of papa and then they would both be after me to beat me up and mama would hide me. Or Butch would run in, blood spouting like from a sieve and I would hold him and I would hear shots and wake up bleeding and crying too. Or I would dream I went with Clara every night and be hugged by men in dress suits and wolves' faces with long teeth. Clara says, He'll turn up like a bad penny. Belle said, Good riddance, I could do without ever seeing any of them again.

Then like it always happened, I was sitting in the park at noon. Two men were talking quarreling and a woman comes from behind a tree and starts cursing at both of them and they turn like to strike her and all of a sudden like always there he is, there's Butch coming kittycorner across the walk past them and throwing away a cigarette, there he is, his cap pulled down and his lovely grin and I am startled all over.

Butch! Butch! I cried running.

Hello baby, he said, where you been?

Where have I been? Jesus, I said, I been down to bury my papa.

Good thing, he said, bury the dead, that's what I say bury them all.

He put his arm in mine. The way I figure it we get hate from our parents, he said. It's no thanks to have kids nowadays. Why do you want to have kids? Look, in a war they'll be shot to hell and get crazy. What's the good in it?

O, it's good, I said.

Look, he said, have you got a couple of chips? Can you stake me to a beer?

O yes, sure. Maybe Ack would charge us one.

It looked better. Everything looked brighter.

We went into the Village. I thought Ack would let me buy a beer on what he owed because I really only had that nickel. I set out to buy a hamburger.

The place was full.

Clara was polishing a pan, I could see her through the pantry window, she blew on it and looked at herself in it. She looked tired.

Gee, you're cute, Butch says, putting his hands hot on mine, you're so sweet I can't stand it.

I felt all my body open in little smiles, like mama was saying.

He starts telling me a long tale about a prizefighter and about a man from Sicily he knows who doesn't like it here, and about an Italian sewer digger he knew who tempers his own shovels because he likes to hear the sound of it. He gets to feeling good talking, and I keep listening to him, but I am not really listening to only the words, something is going on all the time he is talking, and I am looking at him.

He says, Gee it's no use baby, as long as you point those at me.

I didn't know what he meant, and then I covered my breasts with my hand.

Listen! Honest, he says, I'm going to get a service station of my own. We can't get married now can we? But I'll buy a service station. I'm seeing a fellow who knows a fellow's going to loan me some to lease this here service station, then honey I'll be a boss. Trust me, see, we can get married later. You can't get married on nothing, a man wouldn't have no respect for himself doing it that way. What do you say?

I couldn't say anything. I knew I would do it.

13

Clara brought us some beer and patted me on the shoulder and I could see Belle at the fourteen looking at me.

Look can we go to your room?

O no, I said, the landlady—We couldn't go there. . . .

Have you got a buck?

No, I said.

There it is, he said, Christ what is this? What's coming up? What's the score? Live and let live, that's my motto. What's the use of biting the hand that feeds you or letting sleeping dogs lie, but dogs don't lie, not like us, it's just bite with them and shut up. Where's our bite? Are we men or are we mice?

Sh, I said, everybody will hear.

So what? All right. Do I ask you for anything? Answer me, yes or no. Do I ask you for anything?

No.

All right then, that settles that. We'll part. No hard feelings. We'll separate. We'll part.

O.K.

O.K. What are you crying about?

I don't know.

I don't know. My God, that's all women can say, I don't know. Lord-godchrist and the seven angels.

Clara kept wiping the pan till she could see herself, her breast, her gold hair.

We better call it off, he said, go on, have your way, let them hot on you. I know what you want.

O sure, I said, all the men.

All right, let your blood out, open the gates! O.K., let's call it a day. What a day! We had a day no more 'n what a fly does. All right, that's all we get.

Five dams, a man was saying at the bar in a loud voice, they are building five dams along the river. The WPA . . . it's wonderful.

To hell with it, Butch shouted. None of it is wonderful. I don't care about any of it. . . .

Sh, sh, I said.

To hell with all of it. All right, it's nine o'clock. It's Friday. We'll marry and part in one second. With this ring I thee wed, with my body I thee worship with all my worldly goods I thee endow. . . .

He turned out his pockets on the table. There was one nail, a safety pin, cigarette papers, and a fingernail file. There you are, he said, Mrs. Hinckley. The northwest is a rich country. This represents our minerals, our wheat—

Shut up Butch, I cried.

Why don't you admit you're looking at every man in the place? You could have any of them sure. They got more in their pockets for you. The thing is that we're through before we've begun.

I read all the sandwich signs, american cheese, chickenhamporkcoffee-milkbuttermilklettucetomatohotbeef. . . . They looked like signs like love-hatejealousymarriage.

A sign said, Go down ladies, go down.

All right, I'm going, Butch said.

O where is father brother husband? O where is husband for us?

Don't go, Butch.

You can go away, get a good man for yourself.

Where?

San Francisco, New York, Chicago, Cincinnati, Cleveland, Boston.

O don't let me go. The country is so big, so far.

Sure, go ahead. Go ahead weep, you got words for everybody. You can weep for the Chinese, the Ethiopians, and I can go to hell.

Sure you go to hell. You like to go to hell. You've absolutely got to go to hell. Sure you'll go to hell.

Now that's more like it. Let's know positively kid, let's have it, what are you going to do? Say it. Give out. I can take it. Go ahead hit me. I've been struck before and I'll be struck again.

I don't want to strike you, Butch.

O.K. by me, let it go, let's have it, let her fly I can take it. I been on the bench before this. Can't you shoot straight Girl?

I'm not shooting or hitting or striking.

All right, can't a woman give it from the shoulder? Always pussyfooting around. Can a woman give it and take it? That's why I always want to beat a woman down. A man wants to live and not go hankering after a piece of meat all the time, like a hound. All right, I'm going.

Don't go.

If you're going to sit there and cry like a banshee, by God, I'm going.

All right, go!

All right.

Don't go. Where will I be?

Well, where are you anyway?

After all, my papa was a good man.

There you go. That's what I mean about women. Talking of one thing, they bring up another. Who the hell cares about your papa, for Christ's sake? He spawned *you*, he ought to be buried deeper than six feet.

My father planted a longing in me.

He planted a cuckoo in you. What the hell do you want? You want everything. You want everything in the world!

Sure. Yes. I want everything. Sure. I got hungers. I want the earth. I feel rich. I feel heavy. I want meat, bread, children. I am starving. I am sitting here starving.

Shut up.

I won't shut up.

Somebody is playing "I Can't Give You Anything But Love, Baby" on the player. That's an old one. My head is light. I keep looking at everyone, and hearing everything. I've been promised by the earth the greatest feelings, haven't I? I can see it. I can smell it. I am looking to be happy, for a child for myself. I want to be fat and strong. We been sweet and strong on these streets.

Butch, I cried, remember when we lay in the grass right beside the street, with the streetcar going by ten feet away and nobody seeing us deep in the grass, right beneath the capitol. O Butch, you are strong.

He looked at me. O Girl you're so sweet it hurts. We got to have a room. We got to have it.

He grabbed Clara as she went by. Listen Clara, he said, we got to have one buck.

One buck?

Listen, I'll give it to you tomorrow. I'll give you fifty percent interest. Two for one tomorrow, I promise on a stack of Bibles. I'll rob the bank for it.

Butch, I said, be quiet.

You sure are carrying the torch, she said. O.K. kids. I think you ought to take it when it comes. You can remember it kids, stuff like this doesn't come every day. You won't come to no good end but it'll be short and sweet.

She dug in her sock and brought out a greenback.

Here she blows, kids, and my blessing. She leaned over and I put my arms around her and put my face in her thin neck.

O Clara honey, I said, should I?

Go on, kid, she said, remember it.

Come on sweet, Butch said, you'll remember it.

14

I didn't want to ever go out of that filthy dollar hotel room. I didn't want to open the door and go out into the dank hall with the stinking toilet running at the end. And I didn't want to be away from the warm breast of Butch. And it seemed like he just wanted to put on his clothes and get back down on the street. We really didn't have to be out of that room till eleven in the a.m. I wanted to hide, to stay there forever. Never to stand upright in the cold air. Strange in the city to lie prone as if in a meadow along a line of sky, and feel each other near just as flesh as warmth as some kind of reaching into each other, on the other side of accidents and tearing apart and beating and collision and running into each other and blaming.

I didn't feel good. I cried. Butch got mad and slapped me. My old lady used to cry all the time, he said, getting you to do what she wanted. Didn't you like it? Wasn't I good to you? My old lady is crazy too. She cries for something she can't even remember didn't happen. All women are nuts, beyond me.

I hurt, I said. I didn't know it would be like this. Nobody tells you the truth. Now I could see mama and why she was hurt and why she always went back to papa, too, how she loved him in a terrible way. I thought everyone on the street would see this on me. Now I knew what they were winking and making faces about and hitting each other about and waiting for each other on streets for. Even risking their life for each other every day. Didn't mama risk her life every time she turned over and took her medicine as papa used to say. I would hear him say that and I would hear her cry out. I knew now what that cry was. Nobody can tell you.

I felt bad. I felt like I never felt before. I wanted to kneel down. I wanted to scream.

I never had no complaints before, Butch was saying, putting on his pants. I remember my father always in anger, putting on his pants and leaving, yelling obscenities and coming back later, drunk, when he often beat mama, and it didn't sound too different from love-making.

I felt I would never be the same. Something had entered me, broken me open, in some kind of terrible hunger. Some beings, more like hunger, had given me something from their bodies, had come over me, said something—what did he say?—his whole body said something and I cannot remember the words but it would change me forever. You would never be a wall, a closed door, an empty bowl. I could feel my whole front of my body rise like mama's dough, for her good bread. I could feel it heating and rising forever and draw to him, to his good body, to his terrible hunger.

I felt I would put my body down in front of him for velvet, for warmth, for his long strange feet. He was frowning, pulling his sweater over his head. I would always now know the naked skin of man and woman, their heats and hungers, and the awful wonderful need to enter each other, not to be single, alone, hankering. I would know fruits and like cutting an apple open, and seeing the tiny brown little seeds lying together, asleep in the core.

I wouldn't see us flat anymore but great burning balls of fire turning into each other, piercing, breaking, howling, singing, melting together and tearing apart.

I thought of Clara and having it with strangers for a buck and how she said it don't mean a thing if you don't feel it. And how she paid Bill once because she felt it so much and felt she owed him.

It was sweet, Butch and me, he even called my name and Belle says when they do that they love you. It would be good now to have to put down your money and sign man and wife, when the clerk knows you, and to pay up ahead of time like they can't trust you, passing old grinning men and even cops, having a quick one as they say, and it would be nice outdoors with plenty of time and the sun on you.

And Belle saying that about Hoinck, how good he was and how it was even after the terrible years, how good it was for them. And you could always feel it in the Village when they had it good together, as if some great rowdy light shone on us, and some love of the flesh had poured in to liven us all.

Do we have to go? I said to Butch. Can't we stay a little?

You can sleep, he says looking down at me, I have to meet a guy. I'm late already. I got things to do.

What did he have to do? He was nervous. Had it hurt him too? He felt bad.

I held up my arms to him. I wanted to take him back again, I wanted him to come into me again. Maybe it wouldn't hurt so much. There must be something to it beside pain to make people want it so much and pay so much for it.

I felt I became mama and could feel all her terrible suffering and also joy and some kind of giving she was always doing. And when her children came out of her and papa was so proud and then angry. O it was strange and hidden, terrible and wonderful.

Then I saw a strange look on Butch's face, a terrible look.

I was frightened.

My God, he said, there's blood on the sheet. You're bleeding.

15

I came out of that foul old hotel as out of the hole of hell but also the meadows of heaven. I wanted to find Belle and Amelia and Clara and my mama. The street's so known to me and yet so far and narrow, and the walls seemed to be coming together to crush me and I could hardly walk at all as if I had been taken like a chicken by the legs and torn apart. And I thought, What would they say to me and would they laugh or would they remember how it had been with them the first time? Had I failed?

Had Butch won, struck a foul, thrown a home run, made the bases or struck out? How could you ever know? Who would tell you, or say anything, or maybe laugh?

I passed the Greek hot dog place and the door of the German Village seemed closed, very bright in the afternoon light, and I hoped it being Saturday Belle would be making Booya and it would be warm. I was glad to see Clara's great shadowed eye looking through the peephole when I knocked, and she opened the door fast and full open and cried my name in her high bird voice and clung to me like a hungry bird and Belle cried, Who is it? And I saw Amelia with her black hat on, cutting carrots for the Booya, and sitting in a chair slicing onions was Butch's crazy mother, and the steam from the great pots shone from the naked bulb that swung above.

I knew Belle knew when she came toward me, and I buried my face in the great beery breasts and she lifted my face and looked into it and said, Here baby, sit down, you look like a ghost. Butch's mother stopped and wiped her eyes and Amelia cried, O Girl I am glad to see you, as if I had returned from a kidnapping.

Here, Belle said, put your feet up. The blood should go to the head.

When Butch was born, his mother said, I tell you I was nearly torn to pieces, but O he was a beautiful baby, I tell you. I think he's laying out in the sandbox now. Someone should watch after him.

Sit still mother, I'll see to him. Finish the onions, Amelia said.

Have a straight shot, Clara says, that's what you need.

Leave her alone, Belle said.

No, Amelia says, nobody is alone. I'm glad you came here if you don't feel good.

If she don't feel good, Belle hooted. Never mind, the first time is the hardest and when is the last time? Put more carrots in, Amelia, I got all those horse carrots at the market, they're strong but they're good. And more onions mother, lots of onions. Beef is pretty high and dear. Say, I had it good enough my first time, I should have married that guy, a friend of my father's. I was just a kid. I thought he liked me when he sat me on his lap. My luck, the first time and I got into trouble. He gave me a little money and I come to St. Paul where for ten bucks they'd stick a huge vet's needle into you and start it and then you were on your own. I tell you many farm girls died in the slaughterhouses of St. Paul. I was lucky it come out that night and I wrapped it in a copy of the St. Paul *Dispatch* and threw it in the river. O I was lucky.

O, Butch was a paperboy, once he had a big route. Isn't it time for him to be back now for supper? said Butch's mother. How small and worn she was.

Belle was stirring the Booya. The whiskey made me feel better with the smell of Booya and being with the women who knew what I knew now.

I could show you pictures, Belle said, her head in the big steam coming out of the pot. I could show you my grandma and grandpa come from Wales, and a little girl in the door in a starched white dress. That would be me. I never had no child, I've just had Hoinck to mother, and a hell of a child he is.

Then Amelia said a thing I didn't know, that she had had six children already when the strike was on. She said, And I said to my husband that morning it was dangerous to go to the picket line, he might be killed, and he said to me and I never forget it, he said he'd better die fighting than be a scab or live like a rat. I said a raise wouldn't do us any good if he was dead. And he said we didn't live just for ourselves. It would do the other sisters and brothers good, and all the children that come after.

She came over to me and stroked my hair. Don't be alone Girl, she said, never feel alone.

Clara said, I am going to write to Mrs. Hearst's milk fund for some milk for you. When you're in love you need sugar and spice and everything nice. And Clara took my hand and kissed it.

I began to cry. It wasn't only sad. It was for glad too. It was for all of us, so warm, so pretty like fruits.

Amelia pressed my head to her breasts that had fed so many. O, she said, the breasts of our women are deep with the great life of the people.

Now I knew what she meant by the people and I saw even my father underground waiting for the good to come. O, Amelia stroked my hair and my cheeks and my arms, the life that grows in us always coming up, always full and alive.

I put my hand on her belly which was still full like it had live seeds in it. Now I can feel the whole city and how we are together because we know the same. I feel my own little belly and I know the body of all women and even my mama's hanging belly that never goes back in shape.

Clara spins around. When will it be spring, mama? How can we live till summer?

O, Amelia laughs, ho, we'll live till next summer!

Why, Butch's mother says, her eyes tearing from the onions, why the onions are coming up in the garden. Will you open that door, my children are inside there.

Why, Belle says, we steal it every day, we wait for it, I've waited in Cleveland, Cincinnati, Buffalo, Chicago and New York, I can wait in St. Paul till they open the vaults and bring us the seed. If women are to get anything you have to be a guerilla, a thief, a tricker, a clown. O Lord, to be a woman! Well now Girl, you know something we all know. Sisters, don't let the Booya burn. It sticks mighty easy to the bottom and nothing is worse than the taste of scorch.

Later they made me go back to Clara's room to lie down. Come back later, they said, rest. Sleep, they said.

Clara lay down beside me and put her arms around me and wanted me to tell her about it but she wanted to tell about herself. She said she started it when she was twelve with a bunch of boys in an old shed. She said nobody had paid any attention to her before and she became very popular. They liked her and wanted her to say which of them she liked the best. They like it so much, she said, why shouldn't you give it to them and get presents and attention? I never cared anything for it and neither did my mama. But it's the only thing you got that's valuable. Then she began to tell me funny things that didn't go together. Never let a man think he's getting the best of you or that he is boss. They can become very mean and change overnight. She says it's all right if you don't feel anything. If you feel something you shouldn't charge them. Once she said she paid the guy, a Black guy, he was so good to her and made her feel so good she paid him. Yes he took it, she said. Once, she said, she had a pimp. He was always saying he was saving the money she gave him to get married someday and lead a regular life. They even had a picture of the split-level house they would live in. She liked it, kind of taking care of him, giving him her money, buying him presents. You feel better, you feel like the money you take from johns is just shit so give it away or buy something foolish. It's just shit money unless you are going to better yourself.

Listen kid, she said, you got to make that money for the service station, then he'll really depend on you. You have him sewed up. I'll take you out and show you how. We'll go later after the shows and the night clubs close, then the rich johns from the hill are cruising for a piece. You'll look fresh to them.

I think I'm bleeding, I said.

That's O.K., more of the hair . . . it don't amount to much.

O kid, I said, I want to sleep. I did love him, I loved him, I want to help him. I want him.

O kid, that's bad, you're in trouble if you love a guy. He can do anything to you and he will. It seems like they love you at first but they don't, they only want to put it in you. They make out they care for you but O baby, they don't. They'll do you in hell, beat you up, they'll mow you down. O baby, be careful. . . .

I couldn't sleep. I watched her putting on her eyelashes, and all those curls she has on her head and her wig.

She began to talk to herself about her immortal soul and how it was a sin to pick up johns. You will fry in hell, she says, for doing it, and once she began to say very loud standing over the bed—Get yourself out of here before you burn in hell, in eternal damnation. O Clara, I held out my arms to her, you are so pretty you are so good, you won't burn in hell and she gave out a cry and fell onto the bed and I just held her.

16

It was a slow Saturday night and Belle kept telling me to go home and rest. I watched for Butch and he didn't come so I thought he was mad. I had done it all wrong. He would never want to be with me again. But Belle said, No, that's the way men are, play hard to get so you would give them more all the time. Butch, she says, really likes you, I can tell and I'm a specialist. I hope you'll have it good and long like with my Hoinck. When you find a man, Girl, who is your mate, you'll know it and it will be the best thing that ever happened to you and you'll know it all the time.

Clara asked if we could leave a little early since the traffic was slow and she pushed me out into the cold midnight street. You got to get the *do re mi*, she said, for your man. They expect that and then you'll have him and you can get that service station in the country without taking out no loan or him scabbing a job.

I didn't ask, I just went.

It was getting awful cold out, a wind went tearing down the street just under the lights, and it tore right through you. Clara said, You stand across the street and don't come near, just watch. It's not good with two together. A man doesn't like to have anybody watching.

I stood by the University Club and Clara stood across the street. People were going in the auditorium. Clara came over and said it was too early, that we would have a cup of coffee and when the show let out at the auditorium business would be good. She said she would get in three that night anyway.

I watched Clara like I never knew her before. We sat at a table and Clara was looking out all the time for business and giving the men the eye. I felt ashamed. I looked at the table. A young man came in and stood at the bar and looked at Clara. She smiled at him, she knew him I guess. He came over and said, How about it? She said O.K. and I looked at the table and she went off hanging on his arm, smiling into his face. I'll be back soon, you wait here, she said. I couldn't look at her and then, as they closed the door, I looked up and saw Clara so thin, hanging to his arm, laughing at something he said. It was nine o'clock. I sat looking at the table.

When she came back the clock said twenty minutes past nine. She was gone twenty minutes.

Gee, she said, that was luck. He's nice too.

You like him?

No, but he's quick, not like the old men and he smells good and he's young and quick and clean. It's hard now, she said, when so many men are out of work. Look, we'll have a beer. Set 'em up, she said.

A haul that time, the bartender said.

Don't get smart, Clara laughed.

We went out again and I was looking for Butch. I kept thinking he would be in the next block. We parted again and Clara walked slow on one side of the street and we walked down towards the river, and I walked slow, on the other side. All the men seemed to be walking fast in the cold with their heads down and when Clara would stop and speak to them or walk along beside them a few steps they would shake their heads and walk on. One man turned his pockets out and they stood talking under a street light.

At ten she beckoned me and we walked up the hill again and stood by the University Club waiting for the crowds from the auditorium. She said we shouldn't have wasted that hour down there when there was no money. Anyhow, kid, she said, I think I'm getting used looking. I can't speak to 'em like I used to when they thought they was getting chicken. A cop came along the park and she said, Jiggers kid! He went on down the street.

A big fellow, looked like a worker dressed up, came from the river street and stared at Clara and she smiled and walked away down the street and he began to follow. She knew he was following without looking back and she stopped and looked at some green bathroom fixtures and then she strolled into the drugstore. I came up behind and the fellow stopped and he could see her at the counter through the glass and she smiled and dipped her head and he came in very fast and sat beside her. Pretty soon they came out and she was hanging on to his arm and he was holding her hand like she was his girl.

I waited and Clara came down the street and she said, Kid he gave me three dollars and he wants to see me every week this time. Ain't that grand.

Yes, I said. Could we eat something?

Eat is just what we are going to do.

Eating is a good thing. You feel better. Every time the door opened I looked for Butch.

Come on, we're wasting time, Clara says. Hours is short and there's a speedup in this business.

You're not going again? I said.

Sure, she said.

O kid! I said.

We went out and it had begun to snow and after that no matter how far we went, how many men she spoke to, touching their arms, whispering to them or saying, I know a warm place for such a night, no one would speak to her, no one would turn to her; they kept passing her and she held out her hand to their closed faces, their shrugging backs and I could see hundreds of faces of men with beards and mustaches, and lean and fat faces, and hard and bitter, and hundreds of men's feet and shoulders and thighs.

The snow was coming in big flakes and Clara was standing alone. I was so cold, I ran over to her and took her hands. Come on Clara, I said, it's so cold there's no more tonight, come on.

We shouldn't go yet, she said, I only got ten.

Never mind, I said, never mind, come on.

It was so cold and the snow kept falling and we walked close together and I held her cold hand and when we got back I ran in and borrowed some tea from Mrs. French, and I made some hot tea for her, and I took off her shoes and I heated a cloth and wrapped it around her feet and I looked at her like I never had before.

We are growing, in a field that is cold, bitter, sour, and no chance for life.

17 _____

The season had turned to winter. Clara was staying with me all the time now. Often Clara was sick in bed and it was cold in the room so we kept the gas plate going when the landlady wasn't looking, and I put the blanket mama gave me over her and got a brick and warmed it for her feet. And we were eating off her last five bucks. But Clara being there, I had no place to see Butch and he was as busy as a cranberry merchant, him and Ganz, talking all day. They didn't tell me anything, and I hated to see them, Ganz with his good coat with the velvet collar and always after me to be with him. Be with me, he says, and I'll see that you're my girl. You can make plenty. You don't have to go without no winter coat, you can make plenty and not have to walk the streets either, I'll bring 'em right to you. I couldn't stand the sight of him.

Be nice to me, Ganz would say, his oily black head close to me.

You be nice to Ganz, Butch was telling me all the time. It made me wild between them. Something was so dangerous.

I had got desires now. It all broke on my tongue like some wild sweet fruit. As if my bark was breaking in spring, or mama rising in me telling me how the flesh can die, be beaten and lost. I felt a great root springing down and a great blossom springing up, like my hair sprang up out of my skull green, or a terrible root went in the dark with a hundred mouths looking for food.

Late one night Ganz, Butch and I met at the Village.

Your boy here, Ganz was saying, he's all right. He's a nice boy. If he does like I say you'll both be sitting pretty, take my word for it. Take the word of Ganz.

You got a good word all right, Butch said, like he was kind of licking his boots, and he hung his head when I looked at him.

It'll be slick as a whistle, Ganz said. Clerk gets there early, see, eight o'clock. We're outside, the girl here driving, looking innocent as a daisy. You're an innocent looking girl, baby. Butch is at the corner at five after eight.

How much you think it'll crack? Butch said.

Plenty, Ganz said, plenty. Don't worry, we'll all get ours. You think that mewling baby of yours, Girl, will keep his head? He's got to. He moves in while I cover the cashier. Got to time it right exact.

I tried to listen, to remember it good.

You're sitting there in the car, just a girl in the morning. The cop on the corner has red hair, he goes for the girls. He won't have time that early to watch anything but the traffic. I've watched him every morning and that's what he does. If he moves you honk the horn, see?

What's the signal?

You lean out as if tooting for somebody inside across the street, one long and two short. You got to remember.

I'll remember, I said, and took his hand off my shoulder.

Look in the mirror, but don't look uneasy. Look natural and dumb as always.

O, I'm dumb enough, I said, to be doing it at all.

I was just kidding, honey, you'll be fine. Be ready to get away quick. Quick and easy. Surprise, like Hitler. . . .

No kidding, Butch says, how much will she go for?

You mean the girl or the bank?

Both laughed. Ganz said, Butch has got to see nobody but *nobody* gets out of the bank. Think he can do it?

He can do it all right, I said.

Love's grand, he said. I'll turn around and plug him where he stands if he lets anybody get by him.

O, you can count on me, Butch said, looking kind of sick.

Keep your mouth buttoned up, he said.

Keep yours, I said.

I like spirit, he says, talk back, sock it to 'em. Well, I got to meet some important people. I'll see you in church.

After he left Butch just stood there with his head hanging down. I don't like it, you giving him the eye, he said, trying to put his hurt on me.

Why, you told me yourself to be nice to him, I said.

Well, you don't have to butter him up.

I'm buttering him up? Why you was standing there like a whipped dog.

O, I was just keeping in good with him. As soon as it's over and we got our haul we'll never see him again. I promise you, I promise we'll hightail it out of here, we'll get that service station and never see the like of him again.

A squad car came slow down the street.

Jiggers kid, Butch said, turn your back, get in here in the park.

I said, We ain't done nothing yet. I ain't going to suddenly scream. Do we have to hide before we done anything?

Just as good, Butch said, don't let anything show on the street. Don't let 'em get used to your face.

18

On Xmas Eve I was supposed to meet Ganz and Butch in Rice Park. I was supposed to drive the stolen car to get the license changed. There was a big Xmas tree in the middle of the park and the path cut the snow like a knife in a huge cake. Mustn't think of cake or anything to eat, I thought. If I could stop thinking of anything to eat then I could remember it's Xmas Eve. Men were gathering around the black tree, which wasn't lighted yet. Somebody says that the W.C.T.U. ladies would light the tree and sing later and maybe pass out hot coffee and doughnuts.

I stood there about one hour. I had a beef sandwich under my coat for Butch. It was getting cold. I kept thinking maybe the cops got wind of it, maybe he got some canned heat or something, maybe he was in jail. I left once and walked past the jail and looked at the windows. But you couldn't see him even if he was there.

The wind was like a wolf biting at my stomach. When I got this coat at the Salvation Army it seemed like a good coat, but it was a fall coat and now it was winter. I stood on one foot to keep the snow out of my pump where the hole was. I leaned against a black tree that lifted its bones cracking in the wind. Pretty soon it would begin to snow.

Then I saw him coming through the trees. For me he always seemed to have a little light around him. I saw him far down and Ganz was with him and two other men and they walked like wolves. You can always tell when a man is up to something. He likes it. But it makes me feel sick.

Butch! I cried, and he had his collar turned up, and his face was like a pinch to my heart.

Ganz and the two men looked at the Xmas tree and I took the sandwich out of my coat and took the newspaper off. God, he whispered, a beef sandwich. And he put it under his coat and I knew he didn't want Ganz and the two men to know how it was with him.

Men kept coming into the park. Ganz said, We got to wait, he isn't here yet. He nodded to the other two and they moved away and Ganz stood by the tree smoking in the dark.

What are we supposed to do? I whispered to Butch. You can eat your sandwich now. He began to wolf it down.

What are all the men here for? he said.

They are going to light the Xmas tree, I said.

He looked at the tall tree with the black bulbs. Jesus, he said, is it Xmas? They're going to leave the car on fifth, he said. Are you game?

I looked at him and nodded.

You're to drive it into the garage with Ganz. They'll put on a new license plate. It won't take long.

He gripped my arm. Game? he said.

Yes, I said.

We all kept looking at the tree and all the men stood back a little, bending over themselves like broken sticks, spitting in the dark.

I stood as near Butch as I could and a heat like ice made my body steam. His face cracks my heart. I could warm him, I thought. I could make him good and warm.

They're going to light the lights from the capitol, someone said.

For Christ sake, the men said, some swank!

The snow began to come down very feathery and soft. It rested on the caps of the men.

It's snowing, someone said, after everyone saw it. The men put their heads up and brushed it off their coats and bent down further as if they could get away from it.

I heard they were going to hand out grub, Butch said to someone he knew. He seemed to know everybody.

Ganz moved in beside me and I didn't look at him. What about it? he said, I'll give you twenty-five for it.

Twenty-five! My heart stood still.

That's a lot of money, he said, but a jane doesn't hold out on me often.

I didn't answer him. Butch was still talking to his friend.

They're going to hand out grub, someone said.

They'll sooner hand out a policeman's billy, another said. There was half laughter and half unease. The tree looked dark and deathly rising in the upper air to its point which you couldn't see in the sky.

Some tree, Butch said, must have cost a penny.

I want to lie down in the snow forever, I said to myself, seeing Butch and Ganz. Butch looked like he didn't know what Ganz knew, not his kind of knowing.

I was scared.

Ganz said, Jesus what a coat. You could have a good coat. Cat got your tongue?

If it was summer, Butch said to me, it would be better. Maybe we wouldn't have had to do this.

The men kept coming into the park, black looking, like they had been burned to a crisp and their voices hummed. Somebody made a wad from that tree, voices said, I wish they'd spent the money passing out a little canned heat. Say, that's an idea! You might take that to the city fathers. Yeah, bo. . . . Put it through rye bread and it's a honey.

Put what? I said.

What? Butch said.

You put it through rye bread.

You have to have the rye bread first, Butch said. He looks like fear had eaten out his stomach. He looks hung upon himself but when he looks at me a glint of tinder sparks from his face in the gloomy light.

You're cold, he said.

Say, this coat is warm, I said. What do you put through rye bread?

Canned heat, he said, but the jake is better I heard.

How do you know?

Everybody knows that. You got to have a little something to live. Jack you up.

I looked at all the men and my blood ran white to see them standing in the under-darkness, quiet like, each man alone. Hunger and pain rose in my throat and burst behind my eyes like a rocket.

Why don't they do something? I said. Must be a hundred in the park now.

Ganz said, They're crummy, they'll never do anything. They ain't got the stuff.

They're men, they got the parts of men, I said.

What would they do? Butch said.

What will I do? I said. What are we ever going to have? I asked.

It all looked no good to me, the service station, holding up the bank. I didn't think we would do it, I didn't think it would be anything. I felt like I was looking down a black hole and the wind came out and sawed through me. I felt the knobs of my breasts and my arms and a girl only had it once, Clara said.

I couldn't take canned heat, I said.

You're getting goofy, Butch said.

Ganz looked at his watch. The bastards, he said.

They'll be here, the other man said from behind the tree.

We looked at the black fir in the feathery air flashing in the wintry sky over the dead men in the park. We all crouched over our hollow stomachs, nursing our hungers like cancer and never looking at the other or never seeing a way. What were we all waiting for in the cold? The wind started up again, and tore around them, and each alone not seeing that they made a sea of men all alike, that you could hardly tell one man's strength from another's, or one man's weakness.

The clock in the courthouse struck. It got darker.

Then from the post office steps came the sound of women's harsh voices. You couldn't hear the words, an the men shifted uneasily as if they heard the dry call of lost wives and the voices of harried women.

Then the words came out as it got still.

> Born in a manger,
> Dear little stranger,
> No down pillow
> Under his head.

I want to go, I said.

Hey wait, Butch cried, they might pass out some coffee.

I want to go.

Wait! honey, wait!

The female voices reminded two men of something and one of them told a dirty joke.

Butch said, They're dopes. I saw their jackal faces and their jaws hanging open showing the empty mouths without teeth.

The singing stopped. Is that all? the men said to each other, ain't there going to be any grub? Is that all? Hell!

Why did they have to sing it? If I had a baby I would look like a bag of bones carrying a pumpkin. Then bells began to ring from right and left, and it seemed like from above and under the earth.

Well, what is it? someone asked.

Very pretty, a young boy said, but can you eat it?

The bells stopped like none of it had been planned very well, and nothing happened for a few minutes, and everyone just looked at the tree, waiting. Still the lights didn't go on.

I guess they can't pay the light bill, someone said, and everyone laughed.

Two dopes behind us said, Which way is it? The cops'll come through here and bust us up. They began to move in front of the tree and stood there like a big wall was in front of them, and one of them stepped clear and ran into me, and I could see his white eyes and I remembered how in summer they would lie in the park asleep with the flies crawling on their lids like vermin. I guided him to the walk and set his face toward the light ahead.

Don't do that, Butch said.

He can't see, I said.

All right, he said, if you want to touch anybody you see, any old hop-head, go ahead.

I don't, I cried.

All right, go ahead, he said, I'm going.

Don't leave, I said, looking back at Ganz, where will I be?

Where are you now? Go ahead with Ganz, he said. He can give you everything. She'll go with you, he said to Ganz, I told her, take her. You can give her something she wants.

I ran beside him. Go away, he shouted, hold your coat together.

I hung on to him, running beside him. What are you going to do? I cried.

The men were watching us. What's the matter pardner, having trouble with her?

I ran beside him and he broke away and pushed me so I fell on the ground and when I got up he was gone. I couldn't see him and the lights went on, on the tree. They went off again, and the light came and went and showed the thin charred men standing on the hollow stalks of their bodies.

Ganz had hold of my arm by now and I could smell the smell of whiskey and sen-sen and something else.

Is it growing? a man's voice that sounded like a fairy said, and all the men laughed.

No baby, said a deep voice. Alderman Johnson had it put up.

Ganz said, O.K., they're here, let's go.

I heard a horn honking. Ganz had hold of my arm and we cut across the park in the snow and through the bushes and got in a big car standing by the curb. It was empty and the keys were in the ignition. I could see the two men that were with Ganz walking slowly away down the sidewalk.

Ganz said, there's the starter. Throw her in. Let's get out of here.

I did what he told me.

It was cold when we drove away from the park towards the river. Ganz put his arm around me. Are you cold, baby?

I was shivering and the carols got fainter and there were no lights just the cold high air.

You drive good, he said.

I thought I could drive right off into the darkness over the river and we would sink down through the air like a knife and slit the whole rotten fruit open. I wanted to hit him.

Take your arm away I said, it makes me nervous, I can't drive.

O.K. he said, you're the doctor, anything you say baby. We'll really celebrate if this comes off honey, the best party you've ever had and you'll be the queen, it'll be all for you. Is that car following us? Better take a right here down to the warehouses.

Better be hiding, I said, better be running, better be on the lam, better fade away.

Yeah, he said, better not be seen, and I saw his terrible eyes looking, shaking like dice—snake-eyes.

19

Ganz said, In a week we'll be set.

I didn't say anything.

Don't you like me a little, baby. Most girls fall for me heavy.

I didn't say anything.

Listen, he said, that twenty-five still holds good, that's a lot of money.

Twenty-five, I thought. That's enough for the service station, with what Butch can get.

I said, I'll do it.

His eyes changed color. You won't be sorry. I'll be good to you.

Where? I said.

Here, he gave me five bucks. Go to this hotel. Get a good room. I'll be up at ten. You be there, he said.

Yes, I'll be there, I said.

I went home. I asked Clara if she would lend me her best dress. She said she would. She looked at me. She looked bad.

Do you feel better, Clara? I said.

Yes, she said.

I brought you some oranges.

Oranges, she said, and looked at me.

I put on her dress and I put on a lot of lipstick and I kissed her and she knew it when she looked at me. She turned over with her face to the wall.

I went downstairs. Funny, but I thought I would see Butch standing behind the post in the stairway. I thought I'd see him in the street. I thought he would be on the corner, then I thought he would be coming out of Eddie's. I didn't see him until I got to Seven Corners and he was crossing the street, three sheets to the wind and I knew Ganz gave him an advance too. Damn him.

He was glad to see me. It was only six. I said, You want to have a party?

Sure, he said, that's what I'm having.

All right, I said. You meet me at the Russell Hotel in twenty minutes, ask for me, and come up. It will be all right.

He stopped on the street. What is it? he said.

Listen, honey, I said, I do what you say without asking anything. Just once you do what I say, huh?

He smiled. O.K., he said, I'll do it. In twenty minutes.

I asked for the best room they had with bath for five dollars. I paid the five dollars and went up and then I gave the boy a tip of the last quarter I had and he went away and it was a swell room with mahogany furniture, and pink lamp shades over the bed, and big pillows covered with pink ruffles. I looked at the furniture and sat in the chairs and laid down on the bed, and then I turned on the water in the bathroom and I took a hot bath with plenty of water and there were no cockroaches and Butch came, and I let him in naked with soap all over me, and he put his arms around me, and he couldn't hold me I was so slippery, and he laughed and I pushed him on the bed and laid by him.

He said, Gee, honey, this is nice, it smells good, you smell good.

How do you like it, I said, Mr. Hinckley?

I like it, Mrs. Hinckley, he said.

You could see over Rice Park and it was dusk out and we lay there a long time and I drank some whiskey.

Let's don't remember anything, I said.

Let's don't look fore or aft, he said, and don't fall off the raft, Mrs. Hinckley, because nobody could bring you back aboard.

This is fine, I said.

If you didn't ever have to leave here, Butch said, if you never had to go out.

What would we eat? I said.

I'd eat you, Butch said. You're sweet.

It was lovely, the great lovely life he gave me. And then he went to sleep.

The clock outside struck. It struck every quarter hour. I counted them. When it struck four times I had to wake him up. I raised on my elbow and looked at him. I looked at his hands, at his black head, at his sharp face, strong like an ax.

He will be always leaving, getting up from the bed, and going out the door. I saw now in a few minutes he would do this again, get up and go out the door.

The clock struck the fourth time. I touched his arm and he threw out his arms like he was fighting. I kissed him and he put his arms around me. I knew he would never be sitting in a room for long after that. I knew he would be going soon to try his luck, to see if anything had changed. I knew there would be no trouble having him go.

He turned stretching. Hello, he said.

Hello.

It always gets better, he said, it's a good thing to have a girl likes it.

I like you, I said.

Sure you do, he said, I'm some cock now. I sure got to have a change of luck now.

Sure, I said.

He looked at the ceiling. He got up. I could hear him splashing in the bathroom.

Say, he shouted, this is something!

He came out wet. I laid on the bed looking at him the way his chest went sharp into his thighs, and his legs like a strong scissors and it hanging so small like a bird.

He dressed quick. I liked watching him and then he came over to the bed and kissed me and said it was sweet, and then he put on his cap and pulled it down so he looked like the street again, and I could see him forgetting me as he walked to the door and when he closed it I began to cry and then I went to sleep.

When I heard Ganz knocking I said Wait, and I got up and put on my clothes and made the bed in the dark, and then I turned on the light and opened the door. He had Hone with him. They both came in, and Ganz said, Why did you keep us waiting?

I was asleep, I said. I fell asleep.

O, you fell asleep, Ganz said, and looked at the bed. Yes, I said. I stood by the dresser. They stood on the other side of the bed by the window. It was dark out.

Ganz said, All right, honey, and there was a funny smile on his mouth.

I stood there. I didn't know what to do. I said, Would you like a drink?

Good idea, he said, and he took a flask out of his pocket. We'll all take a drink.

Hone said, Go ahead.

I said, He isn't going to stay? I pointed to Hone.

Why sure, Ganz said.

No, I said.

What's the matter? Ganz said.

I'm going, I said.

I'll sit in the biffy and read the paper, Hone said.

I said, What about the money. I want it on the line.

Hone laughed, Well she's a good head for business.

What money? Ganz laughed. I got my lawyer here.

The twenty-five you promised me, I said. I hated his cauliflower ears bent on his fat neck where there were sores and scars where the black hairs grew into the flesh.

Twenty-five, Ganz shouted and they both laughed as if it was very funny.

It isn't funny, I said, I want it beforehand.

Ganz put his hand on my shoulder. You don't know anything until it happens to you. When it happens to you then it makes you different and you can't tell anyone about it but you will act different and someday it will all come into you and into others that know the same thing. I thought of Clara and how all those that are covered with filth and are rotting from the same thing will know it together.

I want to go, I said. I don't want to do it.

Twenty-five is too much, Hone said.

Here's ten, Ganz said holding up a ten dollar bill above his head, jump for it.

I saw the ten dollars. I reached up and Hone put his hands around my waist. I felt the tears sting in me. Jump for it, Ganz kept laughing and shouting.

I felt like somebody was hitting me on the top of the head with a mallet driving me into the earth, driving me deep down and I would never see anything more but darkness.

I'm going, I cried and Hone held me.

Ganz suddenly brought his huge mutilated hand back and struck me full in the face. I fell down, I thought, forever, into the dark earth.

I thought the light would never be so bright again.

20

How much you think it'll crack? a voice said.

Plenty, said another.

How much?

Don't worry, Hone, you'll get yours, you blood-sucking bastard.

I could hear their voices but it seemed dark where I was. I lay quiet like an animal when hunters are near. There seemed to be a light a way off.

The clerks get there early, Ganz was saying. Eight o'clock. We wait outside. The Girl here drives the stolen hack. Ack has another waiting out beyond the bridge to transfer the dough. Butch stands by the corner at five after eight. We have to wait for the vault to open. If we go in before the vault is open then we're done for.

How much do you think it will crack? Hone said.

I could smell them sitting there in the light bending over the map of the Bank of South St. Paul that Hoinck had made. I had seen it before. It was a good map. You could see the pillars and the door and a black space in the back where the vault was and the places marked where each clerk stood by the cash drawer.

Hone said, She's coming to. Get up, Girl. He was leaning over me sharp as a knife. He pulled me up by the front of my dress and pushed me into a chair between them. I could feel their awful bodies on each side of me. My face hurt and black sea washed over me every time my blood drove into me.

O I'll get mine, Hone said. To me he said, If people only knew how square I am. They're always misjudging me. I'm always trying to do the right thing and where does it get me?

O, bull! Ganz said.

When the vault is open, Ganz repeated to me, like a prayer, Butch moves in. You sit in the car. There's the copper on the corner with the red hair. You watch him. If he moves you give the signal. And watch in back for the bulls. They come up from behind now in plainclothes. Watch the mirror but don't look uneasy. Look quiet and sleepy. Keep your foot on the clutch all the time . . . ready for a getaway. Everything depends upon speed with us in there. We got to do it quick and easy, see?

He went on. Everything depends on it like Hitler does it. Know how Hitler does it? Surprise, that's his racket. That's the thing Hitler's got, surprises. The poor rubes don't know what's up, and don't believe anything's going to happen, and before they know it he's over the hurdles with the dough in his jeans, pretty as a picture.

Yeah, Hone says, that baby's smart. . . .

Plenty, Ganz says. I'd like to come in on his racket. What we need in this country is somebody like Hitler, that's what we need. Hitler knows we don't need so many people, kill off half of 'em, leave only the best people who know what it's all about. We don't need all these wops and Jews. God I hate Jews. I would like to snipe off a few Jews myself.

Jews ain't so bad, Hone whined.

That's the way it is, Ganz said. I don't want anybody to argue with me, see? Hey, are you a Jew? he asked Hone.

Hone said, Hell no Ganz, you know I'm not.

Well you better not be. I hate Jews. I don't like 'em, see?

O.K. Hone looked scared. Take it easy. No kiddin' Ganz, how much will she go for?

If we spike the vault and she's open, she ought to come through with thirty grand.

When, Hone said.

A long as no one gets out of there it's all right. Butch has got to watch that, think he can watch that? That baby of yours?

Yes, I repeated. He can do it all right.

God, love is wonderful. Ain't love grand, Hone.

Hone got up and began to skip around the room like he was holding his skirts. Ganz laughed, Speed's the thing, a fast clout, he said.

Speed's the thing, Hone said.

I looked at Ganz. I never hated anyone before—I knew that now. I said it.

What about my friend here? he said.

You're both rats, I said.

All right, Ganz said. Never mind Hone, get you another, the woods are full. But keep your mouth buttoned up, he said to me.

You keep yours, I said.

And I ran out and down the stairs, past the clerk at the desk, and into the street, and I looked back and saw all the windows behind me brightly lighted and the smooth furniture inside and the nice beds. I always wanted to see what they did in there. Now I knew. I ran into the park and I touched the trees and I leaned down and picked up some dirt and ate it. It tasted bitter. . . .

And I kept walking and looking at men and now I knew something. This is what happened. Now I knew it. I was going to know more. Nobody knew anything that didn't do it. Down below you know everything and there are some things you can never tell, never speak of, but they move inside you like yeast.

21

I went up to Butch's place where he lived with two truck drivers. I knocked on the door of his room. I swear I thought I heard him breathing inside but nobody answered the door. I said to myself, All right, if that's the way you want to treat me, go ahead. It seemed I could feel him standing on the other side of the door.

I looked in the library and on all the streets. I'd follow anyone with a cap on and it would turn out to be somebody else. I waited at the Village and every time someone came in I'd raise my face like to the sun.

Then I opened the door of the German Village from the black frost and heard Butch talking a blue streak with Ack and Hoinck and Belle was saying—I'm warning you, if anything happens this time I won't bail you out. . . . They are all smiling in a bad way and Belle keeps on jibing at them the way she does. It's worse than a war. I don't like it.

Belle went on—I got an intuition. It's going to be bad. I told Hoinck that but a man set on walking over a dark pit ain't gonna give no mind to a woman. He can't be listening to a woman but I have a feeling and I'm always right. I wish I was lying in the cemetery with my mother.

Buck up old girl, Hoinck says. Here's blood in your eye. Stop blubbering.

I can cry if I wanna, Belle said, that's one thing is free—tears. No taxes and to hell with bravery.

Ack looks like he is thinking in his sleep, sort of snoozing off sitting up there. When men look like that, Belle says, they're walking a tightrope over a deep pit. Might as well not say anything, just pray.

Belle says, I got some stew on the stove before you go.

Where we going? Ack comes out of sleep. We're gonna drive around the bank, see how many minutes from Rice Park to the front door. Hoinck's gonna drive.

Hoinck drives straight as a die when he's drunk, Belle said.

Who says I'm drunk? Hoinck looked around.

Belle said, Don't worry honey, Hoinck is aces when he's drunk. He drives right through the dark like a hoot owl. You're part hoot owl, ain't you honey? He stroked her arms while she poured the stew.

Darn tootin' honey. Come along, it's bright as a song out.

No women, Ack says. It's bad luck for casing a job.

Every time she passed, Hoinck touched her and she smiled. I knew what it was now my mother meant. Hoinck went in the bedroom and Belle followed and they closed the door. I sat over behind the stove near Butch who was cutting on a stick. We tried not to hear them in the other room.

Ack said, Goin' huntin' soon, Butch?

Good weather for ducks, Butch said.

It's sweet weather for ducks, Ack said. Last year I got a pretty mess of them all right. Some people hunts ducks with a bow and arrow, some cranks.

Give the ducks a chance, I suppose . . .

Don't give nobody a chance—every man on his own.

You never see them until they fly. I wonder if they are listening, setting in the brush. Ducks fly south but the grouse stay.

I thought we was ready to go, Butch said.

No hurry, I said. He looked at me. Ack put his head down on the table. What's it to you? Ack said, we got all night, the later the better.

Butch leaned over and nibbled my ear. I had to smile. He whispered to me. The stove got hot. He began to touch me and I looked at Ack but he had his head in his arms. Butch was smiling and his face was bright from the stove.

Don't be scared, baby, he said. You're a scared rabbit. You got to get over that, sister. All you got to do is know the earth, ain't nothing to be scared of. The moon is right there, the sun is right there. It's right there and all you go to do is not bump into nothin'. Why girl, I got a hunch that this here is all set for us, all made in heaven for us, made to order, see what I mean?

I smiled. I laughed. It all seemed easy. Yes, yes, I said. And I put my hands out, on his head, his breast, his arms.

Pretty soon Belle and Hoinck came out of the room and they looked good. I knew it was good for them.

I dreaded seeing Ganz again, but Butch said he was coming to talk to me. I said, Do we have to do it? It ain't nothing he said, just get those bucks and I'll never see Ganz again. We'll be sitting pretty, he said. And he said, We'll have a place in the country and a kid with roses in his cheeks.

I was scared. Why should he say that, when I hadn't had my period now and Clara said one month was nothing, especially when you had just been with a man for the first time. But I was scared, and now he talked about a place in the country, like papa, with plums and honey. I was running fast and scared.

Ganz is nuts about you. Just play along, Butch said, and it'll be over and we'll have all that *do re mi.*

Butch be careful, I said, Ganz ain't no good, you know that.

O he's all right in his racket.

Ganz is a rat, Belle said, in any language he's bad news.

Well he kept you going, you should talk, Butch said.

Just then I saw Ganz come in. Hello, dope, Belle said.

How are you, Girl, Ganz said to me, coming too close. Drinks on me, Belle.

I poured out the moon and they downed the drinks and I filled them up again. Drink up Girl, have another, he said. He laid out the map I knew by heart by now. I come to get you all to clock the drive to South St. Paul exactly, he said.

Who's going? Ack said.

Well, just the four of us.

Not her, Belle said.

No, Ack said, bad luck to have a woman.

Can do your dirty jobs for you, Belle said, good enough for that. Don't pay no attention to her Girlie, Ganz said, she's just an old hag. Get out of here, Belle said, Hoinck you gonna let him call me names?

Let's get going before it's too late, Hoinck said.

Never too late, Ganz said.

It was awful to see the four of them like drowning men from a rotten ship slanting out together, each one alone but in some terrible violence hanging together.

I'll be glad when they're back, Belle said, spreading her legs at the fire. I moved up close to her, I wanted to know everything she remembered and all the dead and living in her coming up like out of a deep sea. O the trouble I'm having with Hoinck, she said, he wants me to bring in the business and then he beats me up for jealousy. How can I bring in the business and not look at a man? Why did I marry? I could have been my own boss. But get married, honey, it's wonderful. I could show you my mother and my grandmother. Honey, don't worry, a person ought to have a child. I was just a kid, I was keeping house for a dame and her husband got at me. She sent me to the city with a paper with an address. I felt like a worm, I walked those streets, a kid. Then they just shafted the kid and left you to bleed to death. I passed it in a restroom, wrapped it in the St. Paul *Dispatch* and threw it in the Mississippi.

And then she began to weep for all the long dead and the coming dead, all the dead in the earth, all the dead in her.

Belle was a great tomb and I moved into her fat arms and her warm great bosom.

22

I couldn't find Butch and it was cold so I went to my place and Clara's. She had a terrible cold, she coughed awful and sometimes her handkerchief was red.

What you doin' back? she said.

I ain't going to work. Let Bell and Ack and Hoinck get along any way they can. You get something to eat but that's all now. They don't pay the rent and might be put out. That's why they are looking forward to the holdup.

Lie down kid, Clara said, you look real poorly. Take an aspirin.

I don't want an aspirin, I said.

You better take an aspirin.

I don't feel like I was made for any of this. I feel in body so good, I said, so good and strong.

Did you go to the doctor?

I haven't got no money, I said, gee I don't feel like any of this is right, like we was made for any of this. Everything in you is different, looking to something different.

We got to get some money, Clara said, if you got a kid you got to get rid of it.

Get rid of it. I feel wonderful, I said. I don't want to.

Sure, Clara said, but a kid's got to eat. What will you feed it? Be sensible and take an aspirin.

No, I said. I began to cry so Clara wouldn't hear it. I didn't want anybody to hear it.

I must have gone to sleep because when I woke up Clara was fixing her face again and it was dark in the room and something was cooking on the stove.

Clara said, Feel better? Mrs. French brought us some stew.

It smelled good. After we ate, Clara said, I'm goin' out now and make enough for a doctor. She said, Gee kid, if I could bring them up here I'd save something.

All right, I said, go ahead. We'll be put out anyway.

She looked at me. She knew I was thinking about Butch.

Have you told him yet?

No, I can't find him, maybe he's gone already.

Don't tell him, he'll just get mad at you. Next week I'll get enough. There's an old woman on a river boat does it for cheap.

I just began to moan. And then I fell in a terrible sleep and woke up screaming and Clara had gone out to get some money to kill it.

I ran out and there he was in Rice Park talking to some ballplayers.

I've got to see you Butch, I said.

Well, you're looking at me, he said, the handsomest ballplayer in the league ain't that so boys?

I pulled on his coat. Please, Butch.

Well you know how it is, he said to them, the little lady gets what she wants.

Well she wants the right things, they said. I wished she wanted a private interview with me, man.

O hush up man, she's mine, called for and delivered. Ain't that so, baby?

I felt embarrassed and kept pulling his coat.

We went to the tavern on the corner where everyone seemed to know Butch and I knew some of the customers who also came to the Village but we got a booth in the back.

What'll you have, baby?

We got beers and he leaned over and put his hand on mine. It's lucky we ran into each other. I been looking for you.

You been looking for me?

Why sure, I'm always looking for you. I'll always be looking for you.

Maybe Clara was right, I shouldn't say anything, but then I felt frightened and proud and blurted it out. He pulled back like a snake had bit him. Lord, God, it's impossible, you must be wrong. I knew I was pretty good. Rang the bell a couple times before. Jesus. Well, the river woman can get rid of it and cheap.

I don't want to kill a child, I said, mama always said you should never kill a child, having a child was the only way to make up for lust.

Don't you know it? Lord, when do you learn? You got to be cracked up complete?

Don't get mad, Butch. Please.

All right, he says, I show you how to do it and you won't do it, you ain't got the guts, you're crummy.

No, I said, please don't talk so loud, everybody's looking.

All right, let them look, so what? Why don't you get some sense, then you wouldn't have a child. Live and let live, that's my motto. It's no thanks to bring a child into the world now. You have to feed them, they'll die if you don't, won't they? Sure, you have to feed them for years and years. They'll get sick and all that kind of stuff because you can't take care of them. They'll have all kinds of stuff, and then they'll get bombed like in other countries and I don't care what happens to grown people, get what I mean, they can take it but kids is different, what happens to kids is a hundred percent different, get what I mean.

Yes, I said.

You should get smart so you won't be having a child. You got yourself into this. Now you got all the big odors sniffing around. Since you live with that whore.

I won't listen to your foul language, I said. Everybody in the joint was looking at us. The sun was shining outdoors.

You can listen to all that crap off everyone else and enjoy it, he said.

Who? what? Who do you mean, what are you talking about?

You know what I'm talking about.

Lord, O God.

Anybody can tell you anything and you make out you enjoy it, he said.

Who? Who told me anything?

O, everybody, anybody.

Mention one person.

Well, Ganz.

You told me to be nice to him.

All right, don't expect anything of me. I haven't got anything. I told you that from the start, didn't I? Didn't I? I didn't make off to be anything I wasn't. I didn't hamstring you along, did I? Did I?

No.

There, you see. Don't slap your brats onto me.

I don't care, I cried, leave me alone! I don't see why we can't have a life. We don't want much.

No, not much.

O, we'll cry our strong cry, something will come!

Sure, howl to the moon. . . .

Well I will, I said, standing up in the booth, I will.

Sit down, he said, don't get excited. Nobody cares a rap in hell what happens to you, might as well get that first as last. Get rid of it. I could do it myself with a pair of scissors, there's nothing to it. Listen, you are just like Clara, why are you looking at that little dago, giving him the come on?

I began to sweat cold. I wasn't looking at anyone but Butch.

Cut it out, I cried. I could smell food cooking. I want something to eat. I began to cry. I'm hungry.

I haven't anything to feed you, I told you that.

I began to cry.

All right, Butch said, touching me suddenly, putting his hand over mine on the table. All right, don't make a noise, you might wake him up. He's Irish and he likes his sleep.

I smiled at him. I felt like bells were ringing in all my flesh. I felt lovely and quick, laughing. It's not a fault being hungry and it's not a fault that men hate the hungers in women now that they can't be filling them, it's not a fault aching for a child, food, love.

I wanted to warm him.

23

Ganz opened the door, the cold sun shining on him too. He came over and sat down and said, A round on me, to the bartender. And then he said, How are you? to me and I said, All right, and Butch was watching me like a hawk.

Ganz and Butch drank up and they both got up and Butch made out he dropped his scarf and touched my leg and smiled at me. Wait here for me, he said, no matter how long. And then he and Ganz went out the door.

I looked at the clock. It was five-thirty when they left.

You can't sit in a barroom alone after it's quiet. I got desires now, wild, like the dark sweet fruit of the night that breaks on your tongue. How can you sit down now in any room, and mend your stockings and polish your nails and maybe think about your mother, with your flesh like the wild breaking of spring, like a tree after a storm, weighted to the ground and rainwater in your throat and your hair springing wild out of your skull and the strong root terrible in the earth with bitter strength?

It's a quarter to seven. You look at the clock. In a short time he can be gone and back again. I decide to go back to the Village.

Somebody comes in and asks for Hoinck, and Belle says in her full voice, Hoinck went out. He mixed a Tom and Jerry, then put on his hat and checkered scarf and went out. My husband went out. Man, husband, what is he? Why should grief sit on your body like a carrion?

And Butch, wild with longing and anger, weeping in his sleep. He picked up a bottle last night and filled his own glass, and left mine empty and then threw the bottle at me. Then he threw the rye bread rinds from his sandwich.

Ack has been drunk all night and now he is up to no good, coming in with a suitcase full of bootleg.

I am sitting here alone. He has to hate me. The way it is he has to. It is funny how you can stand more than you thought, and feel youself inside get stronger, and taste the salt of your own wounds, and the weight of the things that have happened to you.

At seven Butch came in and when he walked in the door I could see he didn't like anything. I knew I would say the wrong thing. I knew whatever happened it would be wrong.

We had a beer and I said, I don't know whether to do it or not, I had a dream I thought I would have the child, and I would go south in the sun to have it and I dreamed I was looking through a little hole like in those candy eggs we used to have, where you saw lambs grazing and a little house and children playing in the sugar. I said, It's Friday, and I ought to decide if I'm going to do it.

Butch said, I don't give a damn if it is Friday.

I said, Well I could go south and have it, then I wouldn't be any trouble to you.

O, so you're going south, he said, so you are going away with my own kid. I'm not supposed to have even that, am I?

I feel an awful hunger in me. I feel like an idiot with my mouth open and my eyes hanging out. Clara came over.

They were going to do a square dance, she said.

They want to do a square dance, I said to Butch. The big apple.

There isn't enough people, Clara said. Come on, I'll get you a man.

Don't you want to dance the square dance? I said to Butch.

No, he said. He looked so cold and when he looked at me his eyes were cold.

Come on, Clara said.

O no I couldn't, I said. We sat there.

Butch said, We've got to do it with Ganz. A hundred dollars more and I can get the lease from Standard Oil—I can have a station of my own. I can have a station, then we will be sitting pretty.

He kept on drinking. What is to become of us? Why do we fall apart? He sat there so silent. We seem so good . . . what happens to us? We are being eaten by some rot. Why do we give in to it? He didn't speak. It's like it isn't in us . . . like we didn't do it. He just sat there.

I don't want to become hard and bitter . . . I don't like to feel it. I don't know what there is to do. I don't want success like Butch. I want to be . . . I love to be. . . .

A ballplayer came over. Listen, he said to Butch. When were you with the Wisconsin Blue Socks?

I sat there. People's heads kept going by the window. You could just see their heads and they looked like a strong wind was pushing them, yet it was very still outside. It looked as if it might snow. The sky was low down and looked full.

After the ballplayer left, Butch said, You've got to do it, that's all.

I sat looking down at the wood of the table. It had little lines in it. Then I saw that he was sitting quite still, and he was crying.

Don't, Butch, I said.

Honey, he said, you know I'd like to have a kid, you know that now don't you?

Sure, Butch, I said.

I looked out the window across the street. It said Garbo Coke. Twenty percent more heat, lasts longer, no ash. It was upstairs you got it. Some girls went there at noon and had it and then went back to work. The doors have no doorknobs on them, you can only open them with a key, no one can open the door from the outside. Clara told me that. Clara says it smells awful and he doesn't wash his hands.

I suppose you like to stay with Clara because of the men, Butch said.

O yes, the men, O, I entertain men all the time. I'm crazy about men.

We sat there. Another beer, Butch told Clara.

The little pad the beer sat on said, In my old cupboard who wants bones, cried Mother Hubbard, I like Schmidt's! The radio was announcing that the White Sox made a home run. *We won't ever make a home run, ring the bell, beat the race, come in first. There's nothing to it, science is wonderful. Listen honey, don't cry. It's nothing. I'll do it. I'll do it.*

You'll do it, he cried, you don't care for it. You don't want to have it.

Don't cry, I said. I knew he would get mad next.

Come on, we're going right now. He took my arm and marched me out of the tavern. Thataboy, they shouted from inside, that's the way to treat her. A woman's got to be struck regular like a gong. Pull her eyebrows down. Knock it into her.

He didn't say anything. His grip on my arm was terrible. We went down the hill falling in the dark to the river. We had to go across a narrow crossways of two boards and he knocked on the door still pressing and holding me from behind.

An old woman opened the door and seemed glad to see Butch. Mam, he said, I ain't got any money but I'll bring you the bootleg tomorrow however much it's worth. Give her, abort her. Get it out of her.

She smiled. It won't feel as good coming out as it did going in. Leave her here. I'll keep her till morning. Just for you, my young bucko. Always was soft for you.

He pushed me down in an old chair, then he turned back and leaned down and pecked my head. You'll be all right, he said, see you tomorrow.

She closed the door and gave me some wine.

She went out back and I got up, opened the door, walked the plank to land and ran alone into the dark up the hill.

24

Belle said, Tomorrow night this time they might all be dead.

Stop it Belle, I said.

Hoinck was playing poker with three other men.

Cut it out, Hoinck said, and have a drink. Hit me.

I wanted him to quit for years, I'm going to kill myself if he doesn't, Belle cried.

Have a drink, I said.

A fine way to talk the night before a big job, Hoinck said. We got to go to work tomorrow for sure.

Go to work, Belle said, in scorn. She began to cry. It isn't worth it, all the money in the world, it isn't worth it.

It'll be all right, Hoinck said. Play, he said to Ack, go on play.

It'll be all right, Belle said. A thief's phrase.

What do you want? Hoinck said. I take it.

What do I want? Belle shouted. Godlordchrist and the Virgin Mary, what do I want!

Cut that out, Hoinck said, what do you think this is? Because you have a fit I'm supposed to call everything off.

I'd be better off dead.

Stop saying that. What in the name of God, I'm giving you all I can.

What did you ever give me, living in ratholes from one minute to the next. Stop stealing.

Everybody steals, Hoinck said. My play.

Nuts! There must be some other way.

Well you know it as well as I do. Hit me. Go on hit me. We tried that.

We're better off dead and all our kind.

The men slapped down the cards.

Hoinck yelled, Here's a rod, blow your brains out, or else shut up and have a drink.

I'll never shut up, Belle screamed. Look, she said to me, I got him extradition papers, got a quick straw bond for him didn't I? I got him out of jail. I got bail for him. I hitchhiked from Baltimore, Maryland to Dallas, Texas to get him out of the can once. I took the rap for him. What else could I do? I might as well blow my brains out.

All right, Hoinck said, do it. If the women would only shut up.

Sure, say nothing. See everything blown to hell and sit quiet knitting, Belle cried. Sure, don't say a thing.

Have a drink.

I'll have a drink. Sure.

Butch came in and walked by me without speaking. He sat down and watched the game and Belle noticed it too and she said, What's the matter? Tomorrow we may all be dead and he can't speak to you.

He said, Shut up Belle, mind your own business.

Butch said to me, So you want a father and a husband? Well you won't be getting them. Nobody's going to get them.

I stood by the stove.

You want me to bring you something, give you something? Everybody could hear him. You goddamned chiseler, you lying whore. I wouldn't bring you anything.

The men playing cards looked at me.

Did you have a good lay, he said. Did you have to sell me down the river?

Shut up, Hoinck said. We want to be good for tomorrow.

Yeah, you all know it, Butch said, you all know it. I phoned here and you all knew she was lying up there with that skunk.

He was drunk. He would have a hangover.

Butch, I said, Come with me, come on out. I took hold of him and he came with me easy, I was surprised. He just followed me and we went outside in the hall. We stood against the wall and he put his body close to me. We stood there and I thought he had forgotten. It was good to smell him.

Why in hell did you do it? he said.

I felt cold. Do what? I said.

Instead of answering he struck me full in the face with the flat of his hand. I leaned against the wall. I couldn't see. Then I saw his face awful in front of me, as he came toward me and I put out my hand and pushed against his chest and when I touched him I loved him then.

Somebody was coming up the stairs. Don't Butch, I whispered, someone will see. I could see his hand lifted, this time in a fist and it struck me in the mouth. The man who had been coming up the stairs passed us and I tried to look like nothing had happened. But I couldn't help the blood coming out of the side of my mouth.

It's funny to be hit. Nobody ever hit me before but papa. He didn't hit like that. I took hold of Butch's arm and we went downstairs leaning on each other. It wasn't snowing.

Butch said, It isn't snowing, a good thing too. I hope it don't snow tomorrow.

I hope so too, I said. I could see my mouth. It was swelling. The inside of my lower lip was bleeding where my teeth had cut.

Butch said, What's the matter, your mouth is bleeding. He said, I'll hit you again, don't ever let me catch you again. Jesuschrist why did you have to do it?

You told me to do it, I said. You told me to be nice to him.

Sure, go on, blame it on me. That's my fault too. Everything's my fault. That's what my mother used to think. Sure I can take it, go ahead. I'll lead with my chin.

No! No! I cried and we walked along the dark, rotten streets. I didn't know where my legs were and fountains seemed to be rising and breaking behind my eyes. No, no, I cried, it's not your fault. I only thought I'd help with the money.

How much, he said, go on tell me how much?

I hadn't had a single drink but I felt drunk. I could hardly see.

Look Butch, I said, let's go to a hotel.

Listen, he said, I suppose you think I can't pay for a hotel. I suppose you think only that bloodsucker Ganz can pay for a hotel. Well I want you to know that I got the dough, see? I can pay. I can pay my way. I always done that. I don't depend on no one on God's green earth, get me? Since I was eight years old I paid my way in this lousy world. You're not going to take *this* baby to any hotel, you're not going to pay for me. I can pay for my own room, and for my own girl, see?

Sure, I said, Butch, I know you can. I know that. I've never paid for you. I've never never paid for you.

All right, he said, don't act like it's any different.

Before we went in the hotel on St. Peter, Butch stopped by the pawn shop and took a drink.

Don't drink, Butch, I said pulling him. Remember in the morning. You got to have your wits.

I suppose you don't think I can drink either? I suppose you think I can't hold it. All right, belittle me, see? Go ahead, I'm used to it. I'll show this cockeyed world.

Sure you will Butch, sure you will. O I know you will. You're wonderful. You're a good mechanic, you're the best. I know that.

Do you, sweet? Do you?

Sure, sure, I cried, O I love you. I know it is going to be all right.

Do you love me? Honest?

Honest, Butch. O hurry, come on. Sure I love you. Better than anything.

All right, Butch said, that's enough for me. I know when I'm lucky. That's all I need to change my luck. That's absolutely all. I don't need a rabbit's foot. I don't need an eleven. I don't need nothing. Tomorrow is going to be silk. Look, he said, you help me get a picture of this. I stand by the pillars see, until Ganz gets in the side door, then I go in, step over the swinging gate and cover the clerks from the right.

I'll help you Butch, I cried pulling him, we'll get it all down.

And then I felt good. On my own I had done it. I wouldn't tell him until after it was over. I had to smile. I had already robbed the bank. I had stolen the seed. I had it on deposit. It was cached. It was safe.

I had to laugh. It was in a safe. I had the key.

25

We went into the lobby and I stood back a little and he signed the register and then he looked in his pants pockets, and then his vest and then all his coat pockets, and he took out a bunch of letters and keys from his back pocket and then he started over and went through them again.

I said, Gee honey, I forgot you gave me your purse to hold while you were changing the tire. I said, We had a blowout just outside the city, can you imagine, we came clean from Washington, D.C. without a blowout and then just before we get to the city we have one. I put a dollar on the counter and the clerk gave me the key and Butch leaned against me going upstairs and he said what number we got this time? The number on the door was 23.

Twenty-three skidoo, Butch said. Three and two is five. Five is a lucky number for me. Is it for you?

Yes, I said.

We went in and I didn't turn on the light. I laid Butch on the bed and he went to sleep like a baby. I sat on the edge of the bed. It was an inside room with a shaft. There was no outside window. The window led on the shaft and I could hear men talking in the room above. At first it sounded like wasps and then I heard one of them say, we got to be careful. And another said, But doughnuts is sure.

I didn't want to go to sleep because I dreamed about it every night. I could see it all plain. I've read about robberies but I didn't think anything of it. I have seen it in the papers, banks robbed and pictures of a young man or maybe a girl. I never thought anything of it. I can see myself sitting on the bed dim in the mirror. Tomorrow everyone will know it if we are caught. I am afraid to get up and look close to see if tomorrow already shows in the way I am made. This must show, make the bones go different, and the flesh different.

I am to drive the car. We are to meet Ack at the corner of Third and then we are to part. He is to go across the bridge for the transfer. I am to drive down Fourth and stop in front of the bank just six feet from the hydrant and from there I can see the cop directing traffic on the next corner. I am to watch him and watch behind me in the miror and keep my foot on the clutch.

I wake up at night and dream that I've forgotten the shift. But that would be impossible. Then I dream I am paralyzed and have become rooted in the walk, like when we were kids and put our footprints in the fresh cement. Sometimes it is raining in the dream and sometimes the sun is shining. And I see people broken on the streets by an explosion.

It is awful to bear these things at night, and the horror in your dreams of things unknown to you, not thought of by you at all. I didn't think of these things. It isn't my own evil. I never dreamed of them nor looked to doing any of them. Was I evil? Was I a monster in my youth? Did my mother think of this? Who thought of these crimes and hatched them out to scatter our flesh?

I can see dead on the walk by the corner of that building. I never saw the corner of a building like that before. How far is six feet? How far is it from the door to the car, six feet from the hydrant? I must ask Butch to step that many feet for me. I never was good on distance. Distance is very important in this, time and distance. They blow up to big sizes in my dreams. One foot more, one foot back is the difference of a bullet. One minute more, one second less. I can see all this mixed up in time like a movie when you run it fast and then slow, or run it backward.

The voices above said, We got to have racks, we got to have a lot of racks to make it pay. Then the voices lowered.

I lay down beside Butch and he put his arm over me. In his sleep he did it. Some voices outside the door must have wakened me. I was dreaming that it came that moment when Butch was at the front door and Ganz came out the side door with three satchels of money and there were four coppers came around the corner at the same time. I shot at them and one officer pumped an automatic into Butch. In the light I saw Butch whirl, fire at the officer and then fall in a heap. I lifted a rifle and fired at the fourth officer again and he raised a shotgun and blasted away half my head.

I woke up crying and woke Butch. I said, That's funny I never fired a gun in my life.

He said, I hope it's clean tomorrow. I feel better. How about something to eat.

I said, You get it. I didn't want to see those streets again.

There was a commotion in the hall. A woman kept saying, Go on get going, go on, what's the matter. I won't take a thing! she cried, I don't want a thing. Then the man would mumble something like he was moved and ashamed, and then you could hear them kiss and then she shouted, Go on get going get out get going get along, and he didn't want to go. Voices in old hotels at night sound funny and finally he went back in with her, and we could hear them laughing. . . .

Butch turned on the light and killed a bedbug walking up the wall. He wanted to go out and get some beer. It was after twelve. I said, No you better not drink any more beer. We have to be out there at seven-thirty sharp.

Jesus, maybe we won't wake up, maybe we ought to stay up.

No, we got to get some rest.

He said, Have you got a dime I'll get you a hamburger. *I wait at the front, light a cigarette, lean against the pillars like I was just waiting. I can see through when Ganz gets the clerks covered and then I go in and cover them from the other side.*

I said, you put the money out of the drawer on the counter and sweep it into the satchel. Then you take the satchel to Ganz and watch the front door.

Yes, he said, that's right. It can't miss. We ought to make a cleanup.

Yes, I said. We ought to.

Why don't you be easy? he said.

I don't feel easy, I said. I feel awful.

You take everything too personal, he said. Look at me, I can stand anything.

Yes, I said, I'm looking at you. He was still pretty drunk and I knew nothing could keep him from getting drunker, nothing in heaven or hell.

26

He went out for the hamburger and didn't come back for a long time. They started a party next door. They must make these walls out of paper. I lay in bed listening. I thought if I didn't move I wouldn't remember. It was two o'clock. I thought I better get some sleep. I tried to figure things out. I couldn't figure it.

I could hear them through the wall moving like huge rats, like talking rats, very funny. I thought they would look like great rats with long snouts and blood hanging from their teeth. The shooting craps and the loud bad talk went on and the low roar and murmur of men's voices with the cries of the women riding them like birds on a wave.

The clock struck two-thirty and I could feel all this come into me like a misery.

I certainly wouldn't forget, if the copper moved, to look across the street, up at the empty windows, and one long and two short. Yes, I would remember that. One long and two short, you might say that on your deathbed. Last words—one long and two short.

Didn't anyone ever go to bed here? Were they all waiting for seven-thirty, for the holdup? The men upstairs kept figuring out how much it took to start a doughnut racket.

I went downstairs and it was snowing but the black street showed through. I had a cup of coffee and two hot dogs. I only had fifty cents left of the five bucks. I left twenty on the table.

I had only been upstairs ten minutes when Butch knocked and came in with a hot dog still warm in a paper. He was very drunk. He said he had been talking to a fellow who made two thousand a month before the depression. Think of that, he said, two grand a month selling shoes. Jesus!

You better get some sleep, I said, it's near three.

Do you think I can step over that swinging gate O.K.? he said. I'll have to step over it because it will be locked ten to one.

Sure, I said. How far is six feet from the hydrant?

Don't you know six feet? he said. Look, an he stepped it off from the window to the dresser. Not much smaller than the room. I looked at the space. Space could blow up, it could stretch like rubber.

I tried to eat the hot dog because he brought it.

Butch took off his pants and sat on the bed in his shirt, his strong legs hanging down. He was very drunk. His eyes were glazed.

I put on my coat and ran downstairs and brought up a milk bottle full of coffee. Now I only had fifteen cents left. The coffee cost ten with five deposit for the milk bottle. But that was enough until morning.

Here, I said, drink. I began pounding his arms. You got to eat, I said. You got to sober up.

So, Butch says to the air, I am your father.

Father, I almost screamed. Who was he talking to? A step came down the hall, somebody tiptoeing. He was talking in a low steady voice, the glare of the single light bulb fell on his black head.

I held the coffee to his mouth.

I am your father, he says. Go back to the grave, father, lie still. So, he says, my son, it was better for you not to be alive, it was better for you dead. You wouldn't be a white feather, you would have made the big team. Pitcher for big time, you hear me, that's for certain. My lousy old man wouldn't have known you and you could pitch on Sunday.

Drink, I cried, drink.

He pushed it away. I was scared. He kept on talking. He wasn't talking to me.

I will talk to you when you are dead, he said, when they lower you in the ground, when everything is dead.

We will have it, I cried, if it goes good tomorrow. Drink. We will have it. You got to sober up.

Too late, he said, it's against us.

No, no, I said. We're lucky.

Luck, he said, that bitch.

He swore to himself, like a wasp, ready to plunge it into you.

Drink, I shouted, drink. Somebody knocked on the wall. I was shaking like a gourd.

What's the matter? he said. This place smells like a perspiring corpse. Who's been in here? Has that nest robber been in here? I'll kill him!

Drink, I said, You got to be sober tomorrow. You got to be.

He looked at me. If the cop from the corner comes back we are going to be scattered, he said.

Don't think about it. Stop thinking about it.

All right, you stop too.

What time is it?

Almost four.

This time tomorrow we'll be through with it.

It will be all right. Everything will be all right.

Yes.

It won't though. It will be stinking. Lousy.

Don't say that.

Might as well look yourself in the eye.

It will be all right. We'll make it.

We'll be dead.

No, no.

We'll be dead and forgotten.

O, we will live forever, I cried.

Sure, nuts, forever. You sweet nut. Come here.

Don't Butch, you shouldn't. You got to sleep.

Come on, now honey, turn over, turn to me.

Not now.

The man and woman in the other room were laughing in bed. You can hear them strong, through the buggy walls, like grapes hanging in summer, like heavy wheat blowing in Wisconsin.

Now! Now! Butch cried. Before it is too late!

27

It's funny how when anything begins to happen how clear it gets. When it begins to happen you don't worry about it. When you are doing it you don't think about it.

At six-thirty I got Butch out and filled him with black coffee and walked him along the river. The street looked quiet and clear. It was a clear cold morning and it wasn't snowing. I walked him along the river and then he looked better and we went to the tavern and Belle was cooking coffee holding a wrapper over her breast and looking around from the stove, her ruined face frightened in a way I never saw it. What a life, she says, get up all hours of the night. Can't sleep a wink. Here's some coffee.

We can't stop, I said.

O yes you can, she says. It's only quarter after seven.

I gave Butch some more coffee and put a little brandy in it.

Ganz came in the kitchen and said, We can't stop here, it will look bad.

You look bad anyhow, Belle said, you look terrible.

All right, no remarks, give me some coffee. What's the matter with him? he said, pointing at Butch.

He's all right, I said.

Hoinck came in, his hair sticking up. He had a bag in his hand.

You can't use that, Ganz said.

What's the matter with it?

Jesus Christ man, you can't walk in a bank with a satchel like that. What a man.

Shut up will you, Belle said.

Belle, Hoinck said, get that bag upstairs will you?

Drink a cup of coffee, baby.

Ganz went into the bar which was still dark.

Don't do it honey, Belle said.

We'll quit after this, Belle. Don't rag me now, this is a hard one.

At seven-thirty we went out on the street. The car was in front, the one I had driven to have the license changed. I could see in the back, all the guns, rifles and shotguns on the floor.

The men all wore revolvers besides, I could see them under their coats. It made them all look funny.

I got in. Ganz sat beside me and I could feel Butch leaning forward from the back.

Drive easy Girl, Ganz said, like I told you in the middle of the street so nobody can see in and we don't have to put the curtains down. If we get nabbed now with all this arsenal we'd have to shoot it out.

I hope it's a nice job, Hoinck said, I hope it's clean.

Drive easy Girl. Don't break any rules today. We're dynamite.

Leave her alone, Butch said.

Who's talking?

I am, Butch said.

I screwed down the window. There was sweat on my head.

Speed between crossings, go slow at the crossing, Ganz said. Stop at all stop signs.

I could see both sides of the street at once like I had extra ways of seeing. A man moving down the street toward us walking to work struck me like a blow and I watched him. Everything looked so single, so clear.

A nice morning, Hoinck said. It looked like in a show, everything so clear and the buildings looked like they were painted on.

I saw three men talking on the corner. They raised their heads and looked at us. I can see one has a mustache like my father and a thin face. They go on talking. I look back and I can see the back of one's pants come down to a little peak behind, like my father's pants always were.

We came across the bridge to meet Ack where we were supposed to meet him with the car that they were to change to, and Ack wasn't there.

There was a tire store on the corner. Somebody was inside sweeping the floor.

Where is he? Ganz said. What the hell is this, a kindergarten? We drove around the block and back. He wasn't there.

Don't look, Ganz said. Don't gawk.

I drove around again slow and back, and the man was still sweeping the floor and he looked up this time.

Don't let him see you, Ganz said, cough in your handkerchief.

I felt like laughing, I didn't have a handkerchief.

We drove around again and this time the man came to the window and looked out at us, his broom in his hand.

I never saw everything before so clear and flat, as if it was the end of it, as if you could never get behind or around or even remember it. Like there was no place to go into, to hide. It was crazy. I kept saying to myself there's still time. We can stop now. Ganz leaned forward looking up and down the street. I could feel Butch at my back. I could see him there. I could see him plain.

I could see the street, tiny and sharp in the mirror behind me.

The police squad car was coming behind us. I saw it. I said, The squad car is coming behind us.

Ganz said, For Christ's sake!

I said, Sit still, look natural. It's nothing, they are going back to headquarters, around the block.

Ganz was white as a sheet. You're not so brave, I said to him, you're a rat.

The squad car drove alongside and past us and the two tired cops didn't even look at us.

It's a quarter of eight, Ganz said. What does he think this is?

He'll be here, Hoinck said.

Get off this street, Ganz said. Get the hell out of here, we'll drive a few blocks and come back. Get out of here, get off this street, get away,

Ganz said.

All right, Butch said, you can speak decent to her.

To who? Ganz said. Don't be too sure about that.

What do you mean? Butch said.

Be still, I said. There's Ack. I could see him a block ahead.

Tail in half a block behind, Ganz said.

He saw us, I said. All we need to do is just pass him so he knows we're set.

O.K. We drove back to the tire store and Ack leaned out a little and raised his hand. I raised my hand. Stop, Ganz said. I pulled alongside. It wasn't necessary. Where you been? Ganz said, in a whisper. Where you been?

Never mind, Hoinck said, let's go.

Tell you later, Ack said.

All right, Hoinck said, let's take a gander at it, get it over with. It's not too late. We'll get something. . . .

Make it snappy, Ganz said.

The streets were beginning to have more cars. I drove fast. I drove very well. I turned down Fourth and drove slowly around the corner. I saw the cop a block ahead directing traffic like we knew he would be. When I saw the hydrant I jumped as if it was looking at me. I remember the wall of the bedroom. I stopped six feet away. I turned and looked at Butch and he smiled at me. I felt better.

The lights were on in the bank and we could see in clear. The doors weren't open yet. The sun struck across the pillars just like the morning we cased it. I left the engine running. Butch got out easy and just then I could see the steel vault opening.

There it goes! both Hoinck and Ganz said. Ganz opened the door, took out his briefcase and walked around the car, and back around the corner.

Hoinck got out and slowly followed him. Butch was leaning up against the pillar taking a cigarette out of the pack. He looked natural. Everything looked terribly natural. I saw a woman secretary clean off the desk of the president. She had a white lace collar on, very neat. The clerks came out with locked trays which they took to the cages and opened, sorting the bills into the open drawers.

I felt almost happy as if I knew all this would happen and now it was happening just like it should. I could feel my heart beating high up in me. A woman walked by Butch and he looked at her. I watched him look at her.

He put his hand up to his face so she couldn't see him clear. I remembered his saying, Cover your face honey, or I'll see you in the papers.

I saw Ganz inside.

Butch, I said softly to myself, just moving my lips. As if he heard me he threw his cigarette into the gutter, and turned his face, and went through the pillars into the bank. I could see the long hard nervous cat life in him. It was lonely now on all sides.

Now I couldn't tell what time it was, whether an hour passed or a minute. I felt light-headed. A man walked by and looked at me and I thought his eyes got larger.

It was very queer. Not many people seemed to be on the street. The cop kept turning full face to me and then sideways as the traffic went by him. I kept my foot on the clutch. I could see my foot far down as if it had gone to sleep. I couldn't feel it, as if it had been cut off, and was lying down there.

GET SET TO GO, Ganz's words kept going in my mind, GET THE HOT HEAP READY. TAKE OFF IN A MINUTE. SPEED, SPEED, THAT'S IT, LIKE HITLER.

I looked at the street behind, tiny in the mirror. I could see the buildings slanting a little, and darkening.

I said to myself for Butch, Step over the counter, counter ends at avenue window, small gate there, step over it, you're tall darling, step over it. Clerks and money drawers will be in line with you, cover them. Motion them back, give them their orders, keep them away from the alarms. Don't forget anything Butch, and if they hit it and start the big buzzer, remember, that's a lot of battle for us for sure, that's for sure. Be careful. Clean the drawer now as you come to each cage, throw the dough onto the counter and push it into the bag. That's right.

Hoinck has vaulted the other end at the second pay window. I didn't look in . . . the big windows flashed now like glasses in the sun.

A dog started across the street and stopped. He's afraid too, I thought, and he went back to the curb and stood by the hydrant and then lifted a leg.

I turned my head and looked at the door. I could see Butch standing by the door. Now Butch had emptied the drawers, given the satchel to Ganz, now he was watching the door. Don't let anybody in, Butch. Watch it!

A stout man with a briefcase was let out on the corner. A pretty girl was driving the car. She said, Goodbye, father. He pulled down his vest and pushed up his mustache with his fat finger, walked towards me without looking, and turned in between the pillars. Butch saw him too, and when he got in the door, I saw his head disappear like he had been dropped.

Everything was quiet. I could see the bank so clear like it was made of ice with the sun moving a little over the pillars, such lovely pillars.

Another man got out of a car, it stopped alongside. A chauffeur was driving. He got out, slammed the door, threw away a cigar and went towards the streak of light between the pillars.

I watched now like it was something in a story, something I was reading. He went inside and then almost instantly he ran out fast and squealing in a high voice like a stuck pig. Everything on the street changed. Someone was running. I raced the engine. I felt light-headed. I could see the air.

Then it broke like glass all round me and I heard the guns go off, and the repeater Ganz carried, and two single sharp cracks and the cop on the corner whirled like a doll, and then it was still again, with people running.

28

Butch came backward out the bank door. I kept my eyes on him. He came out with his back to me, and he was holding his side. He was bent over and then he straightened, turned toward me and ran four steps, then he turned again facing the door of the bank, through which people were running. I kept my eyes on the back of his head as he moved toward me. I raced the engine and when he was near I took hold of the door handle and opened the door. I held it open until I saw his head and the back of his ears, close to me.

People seemed to be running past him into the bank. No one seemed to be paying any attention to him. I held the door until he backed into it, then he opened it and got in. I could see the streets in front of me and in back of me in the mirror and everyone was running toward the bank.

I raced the engine and when he closed the door I threw in the shift, grating it a little because my foot had gone to sleep.

Butch said, They're both dead.

I didn't know who. I didn't ask him. I hoped it was Ganz anyway. No one seemed to notice us. I drove down to the end of the street, turned down the river hill. I drove fast and over the bridge without thinking because that was the way I was supposed to go. I drove *very* fast and I could see *very* well. Everything looked *very* clear like on a morning after a storm. I was over the bridge on the way to meet Ack before I thought of it, and then when I realized it, I turned off the road and kept going until we came to the country. Then I looked at Butch, he was very white and he was holding his side. I slowed up. Let me look. I pulled back his coat and his side looked like a tree that had been struck by lightning. He was almost split in two, the skin stripped down like bark.

I knew now nobody was following us. I couldn't figure it. I didn't even try to figure it, I just drove on as fast as I could but not too fast. I took off my coat. Put that on your side, I said, and try to stop the blood.

Where are we going now? he said. It don't much matter now, does it, go on blame me. I got you into this, go on blame me, I can take it.

Don't say anything, I said, it makes it worse.

We were driving through flat lands. I hoped we were going south. I tried to keep to the little roads so we wouldn't be seen, but I knew nobody was following us.

Well, you were right, go on tell me you were right. This is a fine end to come to.

We aren't coming to any end, I said.

He didn't say anything and it scared me.

We kept on driving and after awhile he said, We haven't got a bit of the haul. Nobody following us and we haven't a thing. After all that and not a thing. That bastard Ganz made it all up so he would carry the money. I could of just as well had a satchel but he would carry the money. It could of been every man with a satchel and his chances.

He seemed excited. I couldn't keep him from talking. I felt better now than I felt before the holdup. I felt light as if I dropped about a hundred pounds. He kept on talking and I was scared. I thought he was getting delirious.

There was a short fellow at the bar, he said, *in a black mackinaw. He had a pointed nose and he was always having a fine time. He died of rotgut but he had a good time while it lasted. And he said, What kind of a cup is this? The chalice of McCarthy—he was a card—that was McCarthy's saloon, and he said, this is the chalice of McCarthy. I am going to wear a green tie, he said, if I have to bust a gut. I won't buy beer for any sons of guns that are drunk. If you are sober you need a beer—O he was a card all right—but if you are drunk you don't need a beer. He was the greatest gambler in town, used to gamble with Joe Hill and he knew what it was all about and he knew the cards were stacked. He told me then— Butch, the cards are marked—when I was just a punk, he told me that, but I was smart—I was pretty smart all right.*

There was no use to tell him to be quiet now. I had to find someplace to take him. I thought, should I take him to a doctor? I was afraid to take him. It seemed like we were against everybody now.

Now we haven't got a thing, Butch said, after all that, and all that money in my hands, I can still feel it, what we could have done with even a little bit of that sweet money.

You're alive, I said.

He looked at me.

I was thinking, he said, standing by them pillars before we went in, when that girl went by, there was a few seconds there, I could of walked out then, we could of lived our lives like you wanted. I could of walked out of there then.

Don't talk, I said. I kept on driving through the country going around the towns and villages. I just kept on going and then a river came up and I stopped and got out and took the extra gasoline can out and filled the tank and took off my petticoat and dipped it in the river and washed his side, and put the skirt in along the wound.

I kept driving and nobody was coming after us now for sure, and we must have been about a hundred fifty miles by afternoon and the land was very flat and I thought maybe we were in Iowa and it seemed so flat I looked at the sun and turned east because I had a crazy idea we would drive into the dark quicker and maybe get into Missouri or some wooded country. It was frightening to see it so flat with no place to go but into the ground.

I kept driving and nobody was coming after us. Farmers' wives came out and stood at the door. We drove past like lovers. Butch looked all right from the chest up and he leaned a little against me. The women stood in the doors of their houses, and children looked out the windows. All wives are beautiful.

I did everything just like we planned, Butch said, I couldn't catch hold of that fat bastard, he slipped out of my hands like a greased pig. He let out an awful squeal.

I heard him, I said. Don't talk. I'm going to stop now and get some gas before it is dark. Sit up, I said, pull that coat around.

You don't think it was my fault do you? Butch said, I mean the whole mess.

No, I said, it wasn't your fault. You couldn't help it, any of it. Be still now.

I drove into a service station. five gallons, I said. Could we fill our can too, we are going camping.

Sure, he said, going south?

Yes, I said, maybe it's warm in Arkansas. I hoped we were going towards Arkansas.

It didn't surprise him. Yes, he said, good hunting down there too.

He took our can from the back seat. It was a service station built like a cottage, there were paper geraniums at the window.

This is a swell place you got here, Butch said.

The young man looked at us, and went inside.

How much money you got Butch?

I got a fiver Ganz gave me for gas, he said.

Good, I said, that's one thing Ganz did that was O.K.

The young man came out and Butch said again that it was a fine place he had. He looked at us. O yes, he said wiping the windshield. Butch and I leaned together so he wouldn't see.

I put everything me and my wife had into this place, he said, and now the Standard Oil is going to take it away from me.

How can they do that, Butch said, didn't you get a lease on it?

O sure, he said, that's a racket, they make you feel like you got your place, like you're going to be the boss, a big shot. They take all your dough and they got it fixed so you can't make good. You could work twenty-eight hours out of twenty-four, you could starve your wife and kids and throw them in with it. They got you milked from both ends. It's a racket. They hold the cards, you can't win. And when you give up, when they've sucked you dry, they get another sucker.

Holy mackerel! Butch said.

It was getting night. He gave us the change and when we drove on down the road Butch began to swear. I never heard him swear like that.

Butch, I said, don't.

Oh, the Goddamned dirty bastards. They got you coming and going. They got you.

Be quiet, I said. Be quiet.

I had to stop somewhere. It was getting dark.

29

Once it began to snow a little and I was disappointed. I thought we were going south. I hoped we were going south.

I knew if we drove long enough we would come to a river, and rivers always have dark places near them, caves and trees.

Butch got very delirious. In the dark I couldn't see him but all the time I was looking for someplace to drive into I could hear him talking.

Yes, Butch said, honey it's got to show pretty soon. Where are we going? It's got to show soon. What are we looking forward to? You got to believe in the future. I knew a man, he wasn't my father, but he said, Son, I can't tell you anything but you will find out something. You'll learn something. He wasn't my father but he told me that. I wouldn't pay him no mind. I was a cocky buck.

We were coming to some trees and rolling hills. It was nice to drive into them and not see any road behind. I drove as good as I could and not jar him.

No, he wasn't my father, Butch said. *Do I owe my father any grief? Answer me that,* he said. *You don't owe your father anything. Here we are kicked around all our lives, what do you owe your father, spawning you in it.*

He began to sing. It sounded terrible. I cried a little so he wouldn't know it. He began to sing like he was drunk, to the tune of, My father's gone to sea, of thee I sing. . . . This is a dirty day, he said, a hell of a day. . . .

My mother, he said. *She was the darnedest bawler out and had all those lord there were kids everywhere like a brood of chicks. And where are mine? Where's my son? He'd make the big team wouldn't he? He wouldn't be a white feather. Got to take the old carcass somewhere. I sleep anywhere, don't worry about that, I can sleep anywhere. I'm pretty sleepy. Hell nobody'll bother you. One summer I slept in the morgue every night. Now that's a good place. Joe at the morgue don't like to stay alone with all the stiffs and it's cold in the summer, it's about the coolest place in summer, crawl up on a nice cool slab.*

Joe was good shakes once, going for a fare-you-well. It burnt him up. That's the trouble, you burn up. You don't bail out soon enough. I never saw anybody get out soon enough to save his hide. Joe was runner-up. He used to truck around Como and Rice in winter. I'd be coming down driving the truck, all bent out of shape with my kidneys killing me, and there'd be Joe warming up running like a dog. You can't hurt him now. Why should I be quiet? Can't I even speak? He's been knocked over so often his brains are addled. Jock Malone started a gym, that was a long time ago. Once Joe came back to town with a Packard. Boy-o-boy that was something! And then he didn't have a Packard, just like that, and I met him staggering down Fourth with a breath—got a nickel? he hollers. Damned if I know, I says, shake me and if you hear anything we'll split. Found a quarter and we split. My girl wants to go to a show, he says, and I went with him and I slept until a guy came along with a broom. That was another blank that's all. I've got a lot of blanks. I draw a lot of blanks. You gotta have. My mind doesn't

90

register now. Have I been knocked over?

No, I says, you're all right, Butch.

I saw a bridge ahead and I thought there will be a road on the other side going down, to the river.

I know the porter at the union station, Butch said, *he would help us. I know where you can get cheap gin. He would get us some. Five cents a pint, lay you in lavender for a week. And Mabel Martino the check girl is half baked, short and plump, keeps herself fried. It would help wouldn't it.*

No, I said, we're all right.

O, we're fit as a fiddle, he shouted . . . and began to sing. *The bellboy was drunk,* he said, *and started to lean where the old courthouse was and it was gone, the bells are gone now. I better hit the hay, honey. Come down close. This old carcass better get someplace, take this old carcass home wherever that is.* . . .

We'll be home, I said and I drove across the bridge and turned to the left where the road went straight down in the brush by the river. It was a dirt road and I drove very slow and eased the car down the frozen ruts. I stopped and turned off the lights.

Butch said, Don't do that, don't make it dark, and I turned them on again.

Once, he said, *we were coming into Oshkosh between games and there I saw two ballplayers at the bar. One was a guy named Pinkey. It was mahogany beams, pretty swanky. Pinkey said, Hello boy I'm in the big money I'm staying at the Fondulac over here. There was O'Leary and he was in the big money too and we had some drinks. We had ginrickys. Pinkey had pockets full of money, his old man just kicked off.*

Say, he said, *this must be the road to my mother's. My mother's goofy now. I used to go see the old girl it seemed to cheer her up so to see her best effort, this son of Erin. Does it cheer you up?*

Yes, it does. I began to go on slow. Sometimes there are old shacks along a river.

Gee, he said, *I remember it when I was young. I thought this old world couldn't love without me. Honest. I thought men couldn't live without me. I worked up until I was head of the route, I had to be in the alley back of the News at four o'clock in the morning. I thought I was doing a swell job. I didn't think they could get the paper out without me. Honest. I thought I was a public servant. I was a goof. Now a woman's got to give me food, hand-feed me.* . . .

Charlie had three fingers from N.Y. came from Miami by freight. We flipped, Charlie and I had to sleep together, Red started telling about his kids. He was a steel worker too saved money and lived in a house and paid so much a month a steel rivet man worked with a boy friend didn't have to push the bell button often to warn the men below they always worked together Sam fell off the fifty-fourth floor of the empire state. Shouted I'm going down. I tried to grab his leg. All I could do then was ring bells. I had a pretty big funeral. All the gang. I felt terrible. I worked with a different fellow . . . worked in factories. . . . In October I met Charlie again, he was a sight, didn't care about anything but Baby Ruth candy bars. . . .

Remember my brother?

Yes, I said.

Bill was used to it. When he was a punk he climbed the company poles to fix wires in every kind of a gale so the hairs on his belly would freeze from the sweat of his armpits. I remember I met Bill. When I heard he was born I pulled up my didy and went out to give him howdy, and welcome to this mortal coil, and he was growing about one foot out of the linoleum in the kitchen and I was a little bigger than him. We had another boon companion named Sad Eye Morton and he was a bad boy. We were not good boys but he was a bad boy.

Where are you going?

I'll be back, I said. I got out easy and tried to prop him up. I thought I would walk down the road and look in the thicket. I walked down in the light. I could hear the river on my left. I saw a path and I turned off. It led to a shack close by the banks. I ran back and I could hear Butch still talking. I got in.

Butch said, *He was the greatest tipper over of outhouses and feeler under woman's skirts and now he is a bank teller, very respectable, it goes to show. Maybe he was that fat little squealing pig that got out of my hands.*

I said, We are almost there.

Where? he said.

I drove into a clearing where a car had been before.

I feel like my old man's feet that time, Butch said.

How? I said.

Well I was wandering around and the old man was sick and I happened to see his dogs sticking out of the bottom of the bed so I felt them and they were stone cold. The old man's feet were like stones. I told my old lady that and she let out a yell. It turned out he was dead.

I said, you'll have to help me. We are going to get out now.

I'll help you, he said, I'll do anything you say.

All right, I said. I opened the other door. You'll have to put your good arm around me.

Why that's easy, he said, that's a pleasure. Why that's cooperation.

I left the lights on and they pierced the bare winter trees that looked like the beard of a man.

30

When I got him on the cot in the shack his whole side was a big mouth opening and shutting, with his shirt and coat caked in it. I ran down and took off my undershirt and broke the thin ice and dipped it in the water and ran back putting it under my arm pits to warm it. I hated to put it on so cold. I put the cloth in and I didn't know how that mouth could ever be closed.

I went in to get some wood because it was cold. I ran in the brush like mad. Some of it wouldn't go in without the stove door staying open, but that was nice so I could watch Butch by the light of it.

He didn't say anything now. He slept and I watched to see that he was breathing. It was his being so quiet made me know.

Once he said, You better drive on honey, and leave me here.

I found an old stew pot and boiled some water. It seemed like it had been night for a long time. I thought I should have taken him to a doctor before. I must have been insane. Why didn't I do it, I thought as soon as it is light I will do it.

We did everything O.K., Butch said, except for that bastard slipped out of my hands like a greased pig. If it hadn't been for him.

Something else would have happened, I said.

It was funny, Butch said, there was a fat lady clerk and I told her to get down on the floor and when I was getting out of there to the door I almost stepped on her face and she looked at me. I didn't plan it, Butch said.

What? I said. Now he was going to tell it.

Take it on the natural out, Ganz told us, that's what I did. I came out of there natural and nobody followed us, I did that O.K. didn't I?

Yes, I said.

Well just before that little pig came in, Ganz said, O.K., boys, take it on the natural, get out now, natural, walk east, get that dough in the car. Hoinck had one satchel from the vault and Ganz had the one I gave him. The way I doped it, sometime in my sleep, was that Ganz was figuring with Hone to get all the dough one way or another.

Yes, I figured that too, I guess.

Ganz saw the pig slip out of my hands all right and he turned, and I saw Hoinck fall as he was making for the door, and it was Ganz shot Hoinck straight through the heart, from the back. It was Ganz. Hoinck fell by the door. I saw him. He was so big and he just fell like he was cracked from behind. Ganz took the money on the run from his hand so he had both satchels and I took aim and shot him in the back.

I didn't say anything. I took his hand.

I saw him and I shot him. I never liked to look at him from behind.

All right, I said, neither did I.

And he kind of twisted around spinning to the floor and he saw me, and raised his automatic, and shot the whole wad. Ganz could shoot straight, but I guess I got him bad.

93

All right, I said, try and sleep.

Sleep, he said, I been sleeping all my life. My God, do we belong to the human race or don't we?

Some people don't think so, I said.

To hell with them, I feel so tired.

Sleep, I said.

I had found a bottle of whiskey in the car. I put some in the hot water and made him drink it and I drank some. I began to rub his body. The bleeding had stopped but he was spitting blood like he was bleeding inside. I rubbed him all over slow, his feet, his thighs, his neck and shoulders. I thought of everything he ever told me.

His body had been good to me. It seemed like there was everything else bad, and our bodies good and sweet to us. He said, get in beside me, I'm so cold. I got in with him and put our coats over us and he held on to me and if I would move he would draw me back. It was a narrow cot and I felt the fever mount in him. Sometimes he talked serious and I talked to him.

I haven't been good to you.

You've been good to me. I said, The best.

I hate it the way my brother looked when he was dead. I went back and I saw him face down on the slab, and when I turned him over he looked at me.

There was Rafferty traveled and got his expenses paid, two thousand a month, think of that, met big men too. It brings the best out in you, Rafferty used to say, ten years in hotels, the best hotels, give a tip of one dollar as easy as sneezing. I saw his report it was two thousand for one month. What we couldn't do with that in one year even, if we had it. . . . The boy's doing well. I hope he makes a million.

Butch, I said, you know it wasn't anything with Ganz.

I know, Butch said, don't think about it. We're trapped honey.

Don't say anything.

This would happen anyway, he says, the sooner the better, eventually why not now? We couldn't do anything we didn't do. We put everything into it like they say. We shot the works. It was all in the cards.

Don't think of anything now, I said and began rubbing his back.

I haven't done you much, he said. . . .

O you're good, I said, haven't I done what you said, gone with you, followed you?

Yes, he said, you're sweet.

What was I doing all my life? Butch said. What was I doing, what in high heaven and low hell was I up to? St. Peter Street, Wabasha, St. Paul, Third and Fourth and Fifth. Remember Hogan's used to be up two flights and in the back and Rifle Joe's, and Dodo? What in God's name? Three-story stone building, that's Belle's, I recognize that, an old stone building can be sweet, saloon tailor shop restaurant fruit stand hotel upstairs, rubber worn off, a red globe in the entrance, the alley was a blind, remember that. Smell of sour whiskey rotten fruits, horses, catgut and beer. I worked in a hat factory on that second floor when I was a punk, you didn't know me then, I hadn't slept with you then, I was looking for you. The girls used to hang out their towels in the hotel and we bet on how many towels, that was the first thing I bet on, and the machines made a steady-one-two-stop-one-two you got so you liked it, you would jig it, we used to do it.

We both fell asleep. He woke me shouting: *What have they done to us, what have they done to this now? Where are the oats, the wheat, I was sure they were planted. Look, Mrs. Hinckley the wealth of the country, the iron-ore-wheat-with-my-body-I-thee-wed, with my worldly goods I thee endow. . . . What are they doing to you now honey? They own the town. They own the earth and the sweet marrow of your body. Watch out! They'll shoot at you from all the windows and blow up the town!*

All my life there—what in hell was I doing? Who said anything? What happened? Going around those streets year in and year out, boy and man, those narrow dark Godriddendevilhaunted whorish drunken grand streets upstairs and downstairs—oh Christ my God my heavens good morning good evening—with nothing Christ what was it who made it what got us we come to this bad end?

Be quiet, I said.

We didn't mean any of this we didn't think of any of this, he screamed.

I couldn't make him be quiet now.

He talked about other things, some he had told me, and some of it he hadn't. He thought of all the people he knew ending up with me and then he died.

31

I had left the car on a road going south, and hitchhiked back to St. Paul. At first I was afraid to read the papers and then I saw that there was nothing in them about Butch, or me. It was just as if we hadn't been there. It was funny. For two nights I dreamed every night about the bank. Then I stopped dreaming.

I got a ride with a boy who was selling scrap iron. He was a Jewish boy and he was very nice to me. He said that lots of girls don't like to go with Jewish boys. I didn't know that. It was around five when we came into the Fort and crossed the river, which was frozen, and the hills were covered with snow.

Butch's coat was warmer than mine. The boy asked me where I wanted to go. He said he would let me off anywhere.

O, just along Third, I said, anywhere.

But where? he said.

O anywhere.

Say, he said, I bet you haven't got any place to go.

O yes, I said, I am going to meet friends.

O, he said, that's all right then.

He was a nice kid. I got off on Third below the library, by Vincent de Paul's old clothes store.

I hated to see him drive away. People were going home from work and I walked by the German Village and tried to see in, but the windows were dirty and I couldn't see anything but crepe paper decorations I put up for Christmas. I walked back past the store and looked in the windows.

Men kept passing me. One spoke. Hello baby, he says, and I kept looking in the window. In one window was a bunch of old shoes. I thought I would buy me a pair. I went in and stood by a whole counter of old shoes. I tried one on and it was like stepping into another's grief. Let each one have his own grief anyway. I put my old ones back on and folded up a paper that was lying on the seat. I was folding it up to.fit into the sole and I read it—*Body found in Iowa*. Then I had been clean into Iowa. And it was the laundry truck driver I had passed, just before I turned off the road, who had found him. He had been shooting jack rabbits and he come upon the body, it said, in a corn field. They were wrong. It was beyond the corn field on the hill in the grasses.

It was Saturday then. It was Saturday night. This must be Monday. We did it on Friday. I had tried not to go through towns and I had tried to keep going south. Butch had sat beside me in the seat like he was asleep only he was hard when you touched him, and the blood had stopped and a scab shut the mouth.

I was going south but the cold was like the little teeth of Belle's cats' fangs, going into your skin sharp. I had to wear Butch's coat and I had let mine sink in the river.

I was frightened once when I heard a shot but then I saw it was a laundry truck parked by the road and the driver was up on the hillside shooting. I didn't want to hear it. I remembered it must be Saturday now. It was Friday we did it.

I went slow so I wouldn't have to buy any gas and all night along the roads I passed parties in the taverns and you could see the young girls sitting in cars with their fellows, or leaving the music and going out into the fields. I drove along slow, looking into all the windows. Sometimes I stopped and sat in the road but I was afraid of the state patrol. I had heard the boys always talking about the dangers of the state patrol, especially on Saturday nights.

Towards morning the roads got empty except for drunken boys, driving from hell to breakfast, and I drove up a bare hill. It was cold. It seemed nice, the round prairie hill. It must have taken me a long time to get him over my shoulder like a jackknife, because it got light, and some cows came and stood in the corn, looking at me. The grasses were deep and stiff and made a soft shh where I laid him on his side, because I couldn't bend him now, and a black beard had started on his face. I got the blanket, and I covered him, and I left him there.

They don't fit me, I said to the thin woman, I hoped she wouldn't recognize me. I bought a scarf there once when I first knew Butch. It was a pretty scarf, I remember.

There ought to be something as fits, she said.

No there isn't, I said. I can just put some more paper in. I put the notice in my shoe. As long as the paper holds out.

Well, that's a shame, she said, there ought to be something.

O no, never mind, I said, it isn't going to snow anyway.

Well, you can't tell what will happen before morning, she said.

No you can't, I said.

I went out and walked past the German Village again. I was afraid to go in to see if Belle was still there. I knew she wouldn't be. How could she be? Everything would be changed now. I went back and looked in the other window and there were two chairs pulled up to an empty table, like two people had been sitting there. You could see that the chairs had been sat in a lot and the two had met and parted and the table was bare. I felt like smashing the window.

I walked up past the library and stood in the park looking at the tall doors. No one would be coming out. I walked up to Seven Corners past the old hotels where we used to stay, and it was getting night now.

I walked down Third again, and you could see the river, and birds trying to find something to eat in the snow. They looked black. I went into a good restaurant. I thought I would have something nice to eat. I still had two-seventy from the five for gas Ganz had given Butch. I went into a nice place and ordered mushrooms and bacon. It tasted good. I had three cups of coffee. I felt better. I left ten cents for a tip.

I went to Garrick and saw two shows for fifteen cents. When I came outside it was snowing, big flakes that shone on the sidewalk. My paper in the sole was holding out good. I walked down on Fourth and I watched until the guy at the auto park was asleep in his cubbyhole, and then I ran through the cars, and up the back steps to Belle's. I ran up the second flight in the door and down the hall. I knocked on Belle's door. There wasn't a sound inside and I knocked again. Then I gave the regular boot-leg knock and the peephole door opened and I saw Belle's eye looking at me. She gave a cry and unbolted the door, and pulled me inside, and put her arms around me, and I felt her great back and her warm breast.

32

We cried together. The place smelled terrible of the cats. Shamis and Susy-belly rubbed my legs. Somebody knocked for a bottle. Belle said all she would do now was bootleg the stuff. She said Hoinck wasn't buried yet, he was down at the morgue. The relief gave twenty-five to bury him. I told her about Butch. I said I would like to send a shirt and his good suit down to bury him, but Belle said it was dangerous. She said they never suspected there was another car, that they nabbed Ack's car when Ack drove too near to see what was happening, like the fried codfish that he was, and they thought he was the only contact and kid, she said, you sure must have got out of there on the natural. There wasn't a word about there being anybody else, not a whisper except the pig who squealed, said he didn't think the fellow who grabbed him looked like either one of the dead men, that's what he said, but they didn't follow it up, so you're clean.

Did Butch shoot Ganz? Belle said.

I don't know. They all shot. I don't know who shot who. I didn't want to talk about it.

Clara came in. She had on a kimono and she said, O, Girl, I'm glad you've come. When I put my arms around her I could feel her thin shoulders. She lay down on the bed. I could never tell them what had happened. I could never tell anybody.

Somebody knocked and Belle said, Come in. It was Amelia.

Amelia said, O you poor child. I read about it. I heard about it. O the things you been through, I know them. I brought some stew, she said, uncovering a steaming pan she held in her hands. It smelled good. I felt an awful emptiness in me as if I could never eat enough.

They began to eat. I was full but I was hungry.

You're quiet, Clara said.

What is there to say, I said.

All the women looked at me. Butch's mother stood in the door with a witch's face. She said, I never let anyone go from my house hungry. Come and have your breakfast mother, she called into the room behind her.

It made your blood creep. Amelia took her by the shoulders. Have some stew mother, she said.

Butch's mother said to Amelia, You better call Butch, he hasn't eaten since morning.

I put down my stew.

Amelia said, Don't cry girl, don't cry now. I sat there and I didn't cover my face. The women were quiet and Amelia put her hand which was like a root of a tree on my knee.

Amelia said, You are going to have a child now? When she smiled her face broke into many wrinkles.

Yes, I said.

Why, she said, you will have a child and then you will belong to the whole earth.

I looked at her. She was the first person who seemed to be glad of it. I feel lonely, I said.

O stuff, she cried, why you aren't alone now, she laughed, he will dog your heels now all right, day in and day out. Try and be alone now! Ho! she cried laughing, she'll be kicking around like a sack full of kittens in no time. Ho, you are not alone now, whether you like it or not.

You had to laugh. She was so comical peering into my face, stroking my arms.

I know how it is, she said, you can't break people apart from each other and not have them get bitter in the belly. But lubchick, look! we are all here. . . .

Clara said, You should go on and have it now. And it will take care of you in your old age. You couldn't be any worse off, could you?

Belle said, Don't have it taken out.

Clara said, Don't do that. That's what's the matter with me, it gets you sooner or later.

Amelia said, I don't know what it is, something used to come over me. Every time one of mine was born, I'd say I was never going to have another, and then something would come over me, and all I would want was to be sitting on the back porch sewing on a blanket and thinking I was going to have a baby, and then I would get like that and I would feel good. No matter how hard it was for me I would feel good.

Clara said, O, a man can always be raising some dough for whiskey or ten bucks for those pills for an abortion, but no money to have it.

Belle said, And they're at you day and night. You can't lie down in the daytime the way it is.

We're dumb. We're fools, Clara cried bitterly, taking all their filth one way and another, getting poisoned with it.

Amelia said, It isn't the man. A man is a mighty fine thing, there is nothing better than a man. It's the way we have to live that makes us sink to the bottom and rot.

That's me, Clara said, I'm rotting.

Butch's mother licked up her stew. I have to go now, my husband has come to take me home. I see him out the window.

You are home, mother, Amelia said, sit still.

O no, I'm not home. We had red roses on the wall. I seen ropes and swivels this afternoon so this must be Uncle John's house, and we will have to hurry to be home by night.

He don't look like Hoinck, Belle said. They had me through the third degree something awful. It don't look like him. A woman, honey, can love a jack like that and be pretty surprised to see him lying dead as a door-nail in a pine box the relief gives you. You can feel it sharp in you, the knife of a man like him. The fairies and traders they got nowadays, they don't know how to do it.

I got this veil at the five and ten, she said, showing me a long black veil, how do you like it? It's O.K. but it gets in the beer. It makes you laugh to wear a veil like that for Hoinck. It makes you laugh when other men look at you. Lord, I haven't looked at another man for years.

Maybe you'll marry again, I said.

It wouldn't be the same thing, she said. They don't make men like that every day. What am I going to do now? A man like that can make you feel bitter and strong at the heart. I couldn't stand a man wasn't strong and bitter with a scare and a whip to him.

He was mean to you, I said.

Not Hoinck, she cried, don't you say that. Not him. He gave me it good and sweet. The bitterest people are the sweetest, truly sweet. I got him out of jail, I took the rap for him, many's the time. I remember I used to sit wondering if he is dead or alive—highjacking trains, trucks, stealing carloads of shoes. Lord, what wasn't he up to? With a knife gash on his cheek, four on the back, taking off on wild rips, and coming back with the mazuma. And then we would go off on a bat to Chicago maybe. . . .

What are you going to do now? I said.

Belle began crying. She walked around the room. I went out and got me a bottle of beer.

I remember, Belle said, the last time they were arrested. . . . It was Easter. I sprang them, and they came home and slept three days running. I came back from mass and they both were on the bed, naked as the lord made them, sound asleep.

You can't keep on remembering forever, I said. I'm hungry. I'll never have the things I want. Nobody can shut me up, I'm not going to be good, be happy, make plans, act like nothing has happened.

That's right, Belle said, look at Clara.

Yes, I said, look at her. She was sleeping on the bed. She hardly made a mound under the blanket.

If it was just me it would be different, I said.

That's enough, Belle said.

That would be O.K., I said. Others are hungry too. Certainly people are always very quiet about hunger.

I looked out the window. It was snowing. I could see clear across the river. I could see Irving Park and the black trees where the Italians lived.

There are maybe two thousand people, I said, living right out there, hungry.

Two thousand, Belle said, more than that. Everyone is hungry.

Yes, it's so still, I said, you can hear the snow falling.

Ain't it the truth? Belle said, putting some wood in the stove. It was getting colder.

Are we supposed to sit here and grow thin and bitter? I said.

They don't want women to give the show away, Belle said, Hoinck was always saying that to me, women bellyache too much.

I know you can feel wonderful, Belle says. O, I haven't slept for two nights. I had a bad one last night. If I drink a shot now I'll have to have four. O, I might as well take four as one, I take four maybe I can sleep this night. One night more or less.

She got out a bottle and started to pour a shot. Want one?

No, I said, it isn't any good. I could remember this winter forever. I could never forget it.

Belle leaned over pouring out the shot carefully, her head bent on her swollen, fine body. O, remember too, I thought, that the breasts of our women are deep with the awful and wonderful life that strikes and swarms and breaks from us.

I looked out the window at the snow falling. It stuck on the glass. I know I have some feelings and they are mine. The strong young woman feelings, these I know. What can comfort you on these streets? From when I was a green girl and didn't know what it was. I can see down on the walk and people going into the German Village. Belle says someone else will own it now. I didn't know what everything was then. Now I know the whole city and the way it is and the way those in it can be together. This you can't know, or be at home with, until you have lived it. No one can tell you. Now I am at home with my own body and the bodies of others and I will do whatever there is to do.

Gee, it was a cold night last night, Belle said, coming to the window beside me. But not as bad as the day before. Gee, it's a cold winter. If we can live till spring.

O, we'll live till summer, I said.

She stood close to me and her body was warm. She looked down out the window where some sparrows were hopping in the snow picking at the falling flakes like it was grain.

Gee kid, Belle said, they're black as the ace of spades.

All birds are black in winter, Amelia said.

It kept on snowing.

33

That spring was a cold spring. It rained and turned into sleet and still snowed in May. Clara lay in bed all day quite still. They moved Belle out of her place after Hoinck was buried and Ack was sentenced to life. It's life in this state if you are mixed up with a bank robbery, even if you don't kill anyone, if you are even just driving a car you get life, because they want to show how important banks are. Clara and Belle and Butch's mother were on relief, and they all moved into a tenement on Seventh where they were nearly all women on relief. There was only one old man lived downstairs back on the alley and he was very old, but most of them were women and children, each living in one room with a stove and the relief gave you wood, and only one toilet to a floor and running water in the hall.

I stayed with Belle and hid when the relief came. You went in the front door and there were initials on the wall heart-shaped, and dust and crumbs and battered mailboxes and the steps were in an oval shape. It was an old building and had been condemned but now the relief paid the people on the hill a good price for it. Amelia told me a woman who owns the building went to Mexico every year just on what she got from it. The halls were dark and full of rubbish, apple cores, papers, cigarette butts, crusts of bread, old shoes, and once I saw some pancakes that had fallen out of somebody's garbage. There were long pieces of string hanging from the bare light bulbs in the hall so the kids could pull them because in the daytime it was as dark in there as a closet. Some of the windows were boarded up.

You could hear footsteps all day and all night, it was like a husk, every footstep resounded like a drum. Someone walks downstairs and you can hear them walking all around you, even after they've stopped doing it. As long as it is day some sound keeps up but when night comes the halls are dark and damp like grief, and the floors sag down, and the bedbugs walk on the walls.

When you go to sleep you dream people are shooting craps and you can hear a woman next door say, For Christ's sake shut up. I never had a good sleep in that house. In the back, little porches are fastened up with wire onto the wall and you can sit there if summer ever comes. The fire escape stairways go back to the alley where there are heaps of ashes, garbage in cans and muddy water thawing from the black sooty snow heaps.

From the porch you can see the spires of the cathedral and the capitol. I like to see it. I like this part of it. In winter you can see the river and the houseboats.

It beats all how you can hear everything though like the house was a drum and every whisper made a sound, children talking. Quick steps of driven women, a baby falling down. Women cry a lot and you can even hear them when they are still, rocking. Women rock a lot at night.

I was trying to get on relief and I went to the clinic and they told me that to have a good baby you got to have one quart of milk per day and oranges. . . . Well, oranges don't grow in the fine tropical climate of Minnesota.

I didn't like to go home because the two rooms were so crowded with Belle and Butch's mother and Clara in a fever half the time. But it was Butch's mother got under my skin. I couldn't stand to hear her. Belle was drunk most of the time and Clara out of her head and they got so the three of them just sat there with the cats and Belle went out to the relief office to get their order. I was sitting in the park because it was evening and they had put out two benches and you could smell the good odor of bread from the bakery on the corner, and I could see all the people going home, hurrying into their apartments, and one woman came out every evening and waited for her husband and when she saw him she waved and then ran a little, and they just barely kept from kissing right there, but they swung their hands together instead and hurried into the apartment building quickly to be alone. If I got there at five forty-five I wouldn't miss them.

And I saw Clara walking in the park with her good coat on. She wasn't supposed to get out of bed. I was glad she had such a good coat. I was wearing Butch's and Belle gave me a fancy carved belt of Hoinck's and pulling it tight and with tailored coats in style, I looked real good, and it didn't matter what I wore under if I didn't take it off. I wore the aprons I had at the German Village. Belle didn't care, she didn't want them back now because she would never be there again.

Clara passed me this once like a ghost and I grabbed her and turned her to me and she looked afraid. The feel of her arm was just about like a child's and I felt an awful sick feeling in my bowels.

Clara honey, I said, what are you doing out on a damp night? It was very damp, water ran on the walk and off the trees.

She was very excited. She laughed. Cheer up honey, don't be blue, not a thing in all this world is worth a frown from you! Gee, she said, it's a swell night. O, I would like to belong to a prominent family.

Yes, I said, but you shouldn't be out.

O yes I should, she said, I would like to be prominent. I got to see this spring.

I felt cold, and pulled her coat around and fastened it.

You know what? she said. I'm used to the cold, I'd feel funny warm. You know what, kid, I had my fortune told in a teacup, and there is something good around the corner.

Honest?

It was wings as clear as anything in the bottom of the cup, you know what that means? Maybe I'm going to meet a nice man who wants to marry me and take me to Norway.

Sure, I said.

We walked up and back around the park. A car drove slow following us. Gee, she said, a pick up. She giggled and clung to my arm, looking back, her little round mouth open. She had put on her eyelashes too. The car came slow behind us.

You got to walk faster, I said.

What for? He looks like a swell haul.

You nut, I said, hurry up. We cut across away from the street.

You think you are all settled, Clara says, and then your luck changes. And then you aren't settled and there's something different in the cards. It's exciting that way. There's always a silver lining. Something better in the future. . . . Look kid I might see my boyfriend!

You might, I said.

Look kid, I know a swell room for four-fifty. We could get it together. When did you see him last?

O a long time ago. He said all right, if that's the way you feel, good-bye. He doesn't even come now. We parted. Forever until sickness and health, until death do us together, we've parted. O wait, look, the park is dark, are you afraid, kid?

No, I said.

I have sheets and linen and silverware and nightgowns in my hope chest. I was talking to him in a telephone booth and I says to him, just to be married doesn't make a husband or a wife either—at the top of that house there's a place you can rent for four-fifty with bath like this kid, and there's a clothes closet. I'm afraid when no one wants to be with me, kid, that's all I'm afraid of.

Yes, I said. Let's have a soda. . . .

And kid, this place has a thing where the ice hums out and makes ice cream without turning, and a radio. But you know how it is, a man doesn't feel good when he can't work, he doesn't feel respectable. . . . That's the way with Tommy, he felt bad after he had to pawn his tools. He pawned more than his tools all right. It's funny with a man.

Yes, I said. It's pretty funny.

Jesus kid, I don't know how long I'm going to stand it with that old lady, pardon me, she's Butch's mother—but she's sure goony.

I know, I said.

Gee, she's funny. . . . She chews mustard sardines all day without any teeth. Know what she was doing?

No.

She was standing in front of that door that's nailed up and she wanted us to open it.

She says that her children are in there playing and it's time for dinner.

I was silent.

She says Butch and Bill are inside and she's got to take them their lunch. Lordy.

You mean she just stands there wanting them to open the door?

Sure, she just stands there. She thinks the whole house where they lived is on the other side of the door. Nuts. . . . The worst thing is she remembers food she ate fifty years ago. She remembers whole dinners she cooked when she was young.

Lord, I said.

And she remembers her mother and her dead daughter and the orchard where the boys played when they lived on the farm and she'll say, Don't make a noise now, Butch is sleeping. I'll be screwy too. Or she'll come in with something packed in a bag, it might be a sofa cushion, and she'll say she's going home. She thinks she is in another house with paper like this one.

Once she saw a man working on the lot across the alley on the gas mains and she thought it was Butch. There was a black car parked there. She got her hat her bag and coat and she said Butch had come to take her back. She was very happy. Belle told her it wasn't her son. She said Belle never knew her sons, and Butch would not know the house now so she would have to call to him. Take the key out of the lock, I am going home, she said. But you are home. No I am not home, I have to be going now. Open the door. And we had to lock the door to keep her in. And I looked at the young man bent over screwing down a joint in the pipe and he was a young man with a strong back.

We got to go back, I said.

O no, Clara said, not now. We were going to have a soda.

All right, I said. . . .

We went into Walgreen's and had a soda and Clara giggled and talked— made fun of everyone and I felt like a girl again. I felt good. I talked to Clara about having my child. She said, Gee kid, and we both laughed about the oranges and one quart of milk a day, and Clara said if she had a baby she'd just eat spice cakes—sugar and spice and everything nice, that's what little girls are made of, and she might write to Mrs. Hearst's milk fund and maybe she would send out a quart of milk and a carload of spice cakes.

I never laughed so much.

34

I sit in a beer joint now, and I feel I'm living day by day, and understanding some of it. I have no home now. I have no place but the place of this understanding which is a kind of home too. I feel full and heavy and I am walking with my eyes on the street, finding it out now.

It slowly gets to be spring and I walk around the town. I am here, unknown to any at all, and yet known to all. You know what it is to walk in the dark, to have every step you take going down. You get used to it when a street looks awful and the lights and the buildings look like after an earthquake, like they did when I was driving that car for Butch, like when I saw all the men in the beer joint, Butch and Ganz and you could tell they were coming to no good.

You can get so you can go on thinking and living in the streets because you got no home. The streets used to be only something you walked through to get someplace else, but now they are home to me, and I walk around, and walk in stores and look at all the people, or I sit in the relief station waiting to see the caseworker, and I sit there close to other women and men, and I look, I feed off their faces. They feed me. I don't feel scared when I am sitting there and it is warm and I am close to the bodies of others. I don't know them but I know them all.

I haven't gotten relief yet, and I get scared when I think of the days going by and no oranges or milk. Every day counts now they tell me.

We've got a radio, that is, Belle has got one. You have to keep it hidden because if the relief found out Belle has one we would get cut off, so we only take it out at night when it is sure that no caseworker is coming around. We have to attach it from the hall, which is the one place where there is electric light. We play it long cold winter nights.

Butch's mother likes to listen to the radio but she thinks everyone is alive in it. There's an announcer named Mr. Schilling. Will you please sing "Rock of Ages," Mr. Schilling? she will say. Once she heard a baby crying in the radio and she said, How does a baby grow in that shack? I wouldn't raise no child of mine in there. How do folks live in a place like that? They must sit on a log.

Clara got worse because the spring seemed like it would never come and it got so damp. I slept with her and once I found a bunch of letters she wrote about her boyfriend. At first I didn't know what they meant, I thought she wrote them a long time ago, but it turned out she was writing them now.

They were to different people I didn't know.

> Dear Bret: Jack and Bill called in today and were going to tell you something. They said they couldn't trust me with it. Jack looks just wonderful. We are going to get married in the spring. The spring will be here soon and then we are going to get married. Gee am I ever excited am I ever.
>
> Clara

The letters were addressed all over the United States.

Dear Bill: Jack was up today with another guy and they waited for you about an hour. Gee but that guy Jack brought with him was some piano player. They went away in about an hour.

And one letter was addressed to herself and it was in her own hand-writing:

Dear Clara, Jack was here to see you, after you, waiting all that time ain't that the cat's pajamas but I fixed it up for you kiddo all I said was Clara went to the show. He left a swell box of chocolates for you and said he must see you before the end of the week. I will keep your diary for you if you will let me take your georgette hat for Sunday. I am going out in the park Sunday if it is a warm day with that new fellow that works at the Harvester plant, gee he's a swell kid and maybe I'll marry him ho hum who knows? You never can tell what will happen in this old world.

Another said:

Dear mama, Steel yourself. Mrs. Yorey is in the lying-in-hospital on the dangerous list, she is not expected to live. She had a baby but it was born dead. I am very sorry to have to write you this. You know before she went to the hospital the two of them—that man she took up with, I don't see how women can be so bad—had a high time and he gave her poison to drink and she drank it the fool.

There was a long description of a fire in a nearby town that I never heard of, and what a fine time she had at the beach on the roller coaster with Jack, and how two of her friends got married to men who had jobs and were getting along fine, and how she already had picked out a swell overstuffed for her living room but she couldn't decide on a kapok mattress or not and what color should the rugs be? Another one said:

Dearest mother, By the time you will receive this letter I will be dead. Dead do you understand. Give my last and best regards to the kiddies John Emma Vilia. Look out for all your girls, mama, I wish I could take them into hell with me but there is no telling what can happen, strange things happen as people say when you hate a person, when you're dead, why then your ghost comes back and you can take the person you hate into hell with you. Well I hate all the men. What is the use I'll live on again so it is best to end it all quick quick do you understand. Before I will have this baby of Jack's, I will kill myself.

I knew she was making everything up, that she was making it all up, lying in bed every day she made up something different.

Clara said one night, When is it summer, kid? This is going on forever.

It'll be soon, I said.

Belle said, I don't see how we are going to eat until our next order.

I said, Maybe I better go, because I am one more mouth to feed, and it is little enough.

Stuff! she said, of course not. Gee, what would we do without you, kiddo?

I didn't know where I would go.

It was a cold night and Amelia and Mrs. Rose came in, and we put all our wood in one stove, and sat around. There was about four women going to have babies on our floor. Mrs. Rose was going to have a baby. She wished it would snow because then her husband would get a little work. He always felt better when he got a little work instead of relief. He was always gay then and sang a little in the halls.

Butch's mother was listening to the radio. Has mother gone yet? she said. She combed my hair this morning. I don't understand why she left before breakfast.

I sat on the bed beside Clara. She was painting her mouth in a little o, looking in the mirror. I had brushed her hair for her, and when she finished with her mouth, she put her arms around me, gentle like an animal. She looked thin. She nuzzled close to me and I smoothed her hair.

Amelia said, You can't make bones without milk don't they know that?

If they knew, Mrs. Rose said, they would cut their children out with a butcher knife.

No, Amelia said, they wouldn't. You should do something about it. You should come with me.

Nuts, Belle said, what can they do for you?

It's all in the Bible, Amelia said. Under your own tree. Every laborer is worthy of his hire. Every man should be under his own tree and should be paid at sundown.

Mrs. Rose says her man's been out of a job since the foundry closed six months ago. She said, Tomorrow is Sunday. Sunday is a terrible day.

Why? I said.

Belle said, You can't get anything anywhere. You try to have some stew or rice left over.

Clara said, If they wouldn't leave a pressed ham sitting in the grocery store window all Sunday! Last week on Monday an old man comes in and asks can't they give him some of that ham that he's been looking at all day Sunday. Honest to God, there was almost a riot, I'll swear to God, it turns out everybody has got a hankering for that pressed ham, everybody has been looking at it all day Sunday.

Mrs. Rose says, Sunday is awful with your husband sitting around all day too. Sunk in with prunes, oatmeal, sardines and prunes again. A roof over your head the government gives you, three poor meals a day and you sleep. After awhile you don't quarrel anymore, that's a fact, and you don't hate your husband, or anybody, you don't even read detective stories anymore.

My God, Belle said, what do you do? If you don't imbibe, what in the hell do you do?

You eat and sleep, Mrs. Rose said. Sometimes you sweep the floor, but it doesn't matter, and you hate sleeping with your husband because you're scared of having a baby anyway. Sometimes you do.

I'll say, Belle said, and began to cry.

And then in the morning you are both mad. Everything is stirred up in you again. And you pass a window and you stop up your mouth with your hand, all of a sudden you want something. You wake up, you're alive, my God you want something, you want everything, it pours into you. You want a head of lettuce. You think you're crazy and the whole world is crazy. Just something like lettuce, she said, and you feel like making a world where you can have a head of lettuce when you want it.

Well, Belle said, you'll have to just make a baby, not a world.

Ach, Amelia says, who is sewing something for Mrs. Rose's baby. She said she would teach me how to sew. Ach, she said, what the poor suffer for bread and butter, we can't tell even to each other. There are things the poor suffer they can't bear even to mouth to each other.

Yes, Clara says, I know what they are.

I looked at her.

Well, Mrs. Rose says, when you are going to have a baby you got to have it. You can't wait till the depression is over.

I said, I heard of a woman at the relief she went to the hospital to have her baby in labor, two minute pains, and they told her she wasn't registered, to come back tomorrow.

Tomorrow! Mrs. Rose laughs.

No, tomorrow! Amelia cries.

It's got so a woman is crazy to have a baby, Mrs. Rose says. If it would only snow.

The radio crooner sang, I'm in love again, and Butch's mother laughed. He's singing about love, she whispered to someone you couldn't see beside her—They're on their honeymoon, I'll bet a dollar. O, glory!

Amelia said, There is no use saying it is this and that, it is men, it is women, it is one thing and another. We all got to be alive, and not lay down, and *fight* for it. We got to be men and women again and want everything and dream everything and fight for it, so? I know how you feel. When my husband first was a union man I only favored it because he was my husband and he was in favor of it. But when I got the news that he was dead and his brother came in to tell me he was dead, I was different after that.

I listened to her closer now. I am different too, I thought. How did he die again?

We had six children then, she said, *the biggest one was Ella she was eight, going on nine. The youngest was inside me. When he went that morning in the strike, I told him there was going to be trouble, and he might get killed, and he said to me, I'll never forget it, he said he'd better die fighting than be a scab or live like a mouse. I said if he died the raise wouldn't do him no good. He said it would do the others some good. He said it would do the other union men good, and he wasn't no man if he didn't stand up and fight with the others.*

It's beginning to snow, Mrs. Rose said, looking out the window. Big white flakes like faces looked in the window.

I didn't think scabs were he-men nohow, she went on, *they don't hold up for their rights. I figure a man who don't hold up for his rights is no man nohow. Woman either. That goes double for women.*

The fire burned hot. I put in another stick. We had seven sticks left. After that we would have to go to bed to be warm. People began to come in, doors slammed below. The snow was falling. Everybody talks about their lives this time of night.

We could have some hot water, Belle said, with a little milk in it. There was about a quarter finger of whiskey in her bottle. She went to get the milk off the windowsill. Is this all the milk? she said. Amelia looked funny, and she began crying in a loud voice, All the milk, my God, everybody knows you can't make bones out of water, doesn't everybody know that. I took that new woman next door a little milk. A woman can't make bones without the stuff to make it in her.

Sit down, Belle said. It's all right. Drink your pink tea. . . .

Look, Mrs. Rose says, it's snowing. There will be some shoveling to do.

I looked out the window. The feathery flakes came down white and melted as fast as they fell on the roofs and walks. I could see far below, the wet street. It would have to snow a long time before it made any shoveling.

Milk went up two cents today, Amelia said. Milk is dearer.

35

Amelia has been telling me things for a long time and now it gets clearer and clearer, yes clearer. The dicks follow you and the policematrons are trying to get some dirt on you. This woman, I found out later her name was Bradley, would be following me like a shadow. I would go to buy groceries for Belle, and I would turn my head, and my blood would stop right in my skin, there she would be standing looking at me. She's a stool and why should she be following me around?

I was going into the five and ten, and there she was with a dick standing by the hot dog stand, kind of looking above my head, but she didn't fool me. I stood around and then I beat it out. The next day I went to the relief and there was Anna Bradley sitting right behind me. I don't know if she came in after me. I didn't see her till I was sitting there about ten minutes and then someone was kind of kicking the bottom of my chair and I turned around and sure as shooting there it was Anna Bradley large as life and twice as bright. She kept kicking my seat with her high-faluting high-heeled shoes and her old face made up for the kill and she sat there and went in right ahead of me to see Miss Rice and I knew then she was maybe going to tell her something. Maybe she was going to lie and tell her I went to that house when I didn't. I could feel my skin shrivel and I sweated thinking now she'll take the food right out of my mouth.

I went in next and I says the minute I sat down at Miss Rice's desk, I said, What did that woman say about me? You know what she is, I says and my face got so hot like fire was burning within an inch of it. And she says, Well we don't pay no attention to any gossip or what one person says about another in here, she says, but I think I will have to give you only four-eighty this month for food. Jesus Christ who can keep their skin alive on four-eighty a month for food, you can't buy chicken feed, you couldn't fatten a chicken on it. Then Miss Rice says, holding up a paper like she was reading something very serious, and her tight little mug gets very serious, you know, she says as if reading from the paper that if you live with a man you ain't married to then you won't get relief, we can't have any immorality around here she says, still studying the piece of paper.

Honest I shook and my thighs stuck together and I could feel the water run out of my armpits just like I was squeezed together and I said, Jesus I don't go with anybody.

Well, she says, all right but you'll have to be mighty careful, she says and I says, well I will. Does that mean I can't never be talking to any man? Well no, she says, I wouldn't say that, but still it might not be a bad idea you know, girls like you got to be mighty careful, she says, men will take an advantage over you, she says.

Just then the telephone rang and the paper she had fell down on the floor and I picked it up for her, and it was a blank sheet of paper. There was nothing on it at all. I looked at her and she looked at me and I knew we were enemies.

Amelia told me a lot, Amelia is an old worker. A worker gets old quick. I will get old pretty quick. That's why I like to talk with her, she makes things go together, for instance like about this Anna Bradley. I says to her, Why should she be following me around? Amelia says she knew Bradley for a long time, and she was a well-known whore, she ran a house you know, a regular house on the north side. I says, she's an old woman and don't look to me any good for a man, but Amelia says, Well you see even them, even the Anna Bradleys, they was only using them, she says, they're workers too, they're right sorry women, she says, even if they are in with the dicks and get a few dollars a day for following up girls, they're right tragic women.

I believe it after Amelia says it, although I was mad as hops at Bradley for always being there with her rouged up mug and her black dress, always following and following me. She gave me the willys following me around everywhere I turn, walking along feeling right good in me, and the morning real good, thinking to buy me a bunch of carrots or a head of green cabbage, and there I see her and my blood freezes right in my body, and the sweat comes in my hands and feet because I am scared, and there she is looking right above my head.

Besides, Amelia says, they're kind of tired, having so many on relief I guess, you know what with about twelve hundred more girls going on every month. They ain't so particular what kind of work you're doing. Maybe they'd kind of like to have you go in with Anna Bradley in her bad house.

I got mad then, I said that Miss Rice on relief would never want a girl to go into a house or on the streets, that she was very particular, that they followed me around just to see I wasn't a bad girl. At that Amelia kind of laughed. She says, You better come with your own people, she says, you better come down to the alliance with me, she says, with your own people, they're the only ones that care a tinker's damn about you Girl, your own people.

But I don't pay her no mind.

The first thing Miss Rice said to me next time I went in there, she said, You've been immoral, you're starting early. I sat there and she asked me all those questions, Have you slept with a man? I thought maybe she believed in the Virgin Mary. When I told her yes, she said, You've been immoral. I sat there while she was asking me those questions, Have you slept with a man or a boy? Are you married? Now tell me the truth, we want to help you. At first I told her everything wrong. I told her my mother and father were dead and husband was dead. He died in California, I said, in the ocean. She didn't believe a word I said. She wormed and wormed at me like in a sore tooth, and then she told me she was my friend, she told me she knew I was lonely and afraid, and was going to face the greatest ordeal a woman could face, sacred motherhood, she said, and I needed a woman friend. I won't tell anyone, she said, this will be between the two of us, this will be just between friends. And I believed her and I was lonely and told her everything except about Butch being shot in the holdup.

The next day at last I got in. Amelia said I would get in and sure enough when I came in Miss Rice opened her window and called out for me and I went in right at once. She said, Wait a minute I'll be right back, and I looked around to see if that Bradley woman was around, and I saw a paper on her desk and it had my name on it at the top and I read it.

It said, *The girl is maladjusted, emotionally unstable, and a difficult problem to approach. A most unfortunate situation. A change of environment would be helpful, with continuous casework follow-up, to inspire poise, and educational interests should be encouraged as a solution. In our opinion there should be a referral to a psychiatric clinic if she shows indications of further or aggravated mental and emotional disturbance. She should be tested for sterilization after her baby is born. In our opinion sterilization would be advisable.*

I read it three times and then I heard somebody coming and I sat down in my chair at the side of the desk and I felt cold as ice.

Miss Rice came in and smiled at me. Maybe if she hadn't smiled it would have been all right. Maybe if she hadn't said, I'm your friend, it's just between us. Maybe if she hadn't handed me that paper right at that moment and said, Just a little routine matter, we want you to sign this, and I saw the word *sterilization* on it, and we want to give you some tests, she said, just a routine matter.

I looked around at all the people at the desks talking to interviewers, and I knew how their knees stuck together, and the palms of their hands were wet and their tongues swelled in their mouths to be telling what you never tell anyone, and all of a sudden I started running screaming. I wanted to get out of there away from all those eyes looking at my stomach. I don't know what made me do it, but I began to shout, and I never swore in my life before. I couldn't find my way out and I bumped into desks and two cops took hold of my arms and twisted them behind and dragged me out to the Black Maria.

I could see Fourth Street from the barred windows, then the library, and a cop was sitting beside me. He said, Whatsa matter sister, been a naughty girl? He came close to me and put his big hand under my skirt and said something awful, and I began to hit him with my fists until he held both my hands and began kissing me, and I bit and kicked, and then I remembered something Butch told me once, and I kicked him as hard as I could in the groin, and he yelled, and lifted his doubled-up fist and struck me.

And I passed out.

When I came to I saw a cold light coming through barred windows and I thought I was in jail but then I saw a thin girl with a swollen belly, sitting on a cot across the aisle, just big enough for a person to walk, and she was writing something in a notebook. I watched her for a long time as it got darker in the room. My face hurt, my arms hurt. It's a funny thing to be beaten up. At first you don't think it's your body, you think you feel bad, but think it's not your feelings and then you find out it's your body, and you ache all over, and the first thing I thought of was, I lost my baby, and I put my hand there, and I felt it move slow like a fish under water, like a fin moving.

I felt better and I watched the girl writing. She was so thin with a high forehead and a thin neck and full lips and her body swelled down like a vase, and I knew she was going to have a child too.

I said, Where is this? And she kept on writing. I said, Where is this? And she looked out the window and put the tip of her pencil to her full lips. I reached out and touched her and she looked at me sudden, with pleasure and smiled and nodded at me but she did not speak. I asked her again and she laughed and shook her head as if I offered her something she could not take, and then she began to write, looking at me all the time with bright eyes, signaling for me to wait for her, and she handed me the paper, and it said,

I am deaf.

I looked at her and she smiled and I wrote on the pad.

Where am I?

And I waited while she wrote and I saw her hair curl so thin on her head down her neck that looked like it wouldn't hold her head up.

What I read was, *The relief maternity home. . . . I'm gonna pop soon. When do you pop?*

36

There was one bathroom that said, "Syphilitics Only," and the other said, "Non-Syphilitics Only." They told me to stay in my room, that I could only go to the bathroom and to the non-syphilitic one, and the matron said, So far.

The girls looked in at me and sometimes they came in and asked what was I in for? How did it look outside? When was I going to pop? When they came in they had to watch for the matron and run when she was coming up the stairs. Alice, the deaf girl, and I wrote notes and looked out the black bars at the snow.

In the cold mornings I could see the girls about to deliver walk slow down the hall. Every night you could hear screams from someone in labor, and day and night the kids squalled in the nursery and the girls would go down the halls trying to see their babies, but they couldn't.

At night the policewoman sat up all night at the bottom of the stairs. Every half hour she went through the halls with a flashlight. She was a great strong woman and the girls said she pinched and bent your arms when she got hold of you.

I couldn't sleep in there for thinking they would sterilize me. When I went to the bathroom and back I could see in the open doors and the beds would be drawn close together and I could hear the girls laughing and whispering.

Alice said there were electric alarms at the windows. There was certainly no way to be escaping. I couldn't sleep so I began dreaming about the inside of the bank again and it would make me very sick and I would vomit. I asked the matron for a doctor because I didn't want to lose Butch's baby but she said, You are all right, there is nothing the matter with you, you just want to get out of working in the laundry.

Alice told me that somebody was leaving the next day and I wrote a letter to Amelia, and this girl I didn't know took it out for me, and in about two days I got an answer from Amelia. I read it over and over and I showed it to Alice who knew Amelia. It seems everybody knew her.

The letter said:

> Don't be afraid, baby. U are a maker now. U are going to have a good child, very good child, young dater or son. The day is near. Take hope, comrade. Dr. will see u soon. We see to that. Take sum hope. Workers Alliance meet nex day frum this. Have, child, happy, demand ther be no so bad misry for our peepl like we hev so we can hev our childs in gret city with sum joy. See u very soon, deerhart.
>
> Amelia

On Easter we had chicken for dinner and we could stay downstairs one hour longer and talk. There were hundreds of funny papers for us to read, sent by some woman's club, and also jigsaw puzzles. Alice showed me all the people, writing funny things on her pad. There was a pretty girl with blonde hair named Julia who made all the jokes. She said last Easter she spent in a beer joint getting stiff with a guy she had never seen before. Couldn't we have a swell time, she said, if we could push all the tables together and have a beer and something to spike it, with a couple of cartons of cigs, we wouldn't even need any tails.

The radio played "I Love You Truly," and everyone laughed, and a girl who had one glass eye for the one she lost in a munition factory said, You son of a bitch if you loved me truly I wouldn't be here. We all laughed. It was very funny.

I'll be glad to get out of here, Julia said, I'll be glad to say goodbye to this. She said to me very polite, I hope you have your kid here, I think we're gonna pop about the same time.

We'll all go nuts together in this joint, the girl with the glass eye said bitterly.

When are you going to deliver? I asked her.

Hell, she said, if you work nine hours a day and no fresh air, you're too damned tired to deliver.

A girl with yellow hair like straw came in and everyone was quiet.

Alice wrote on the pad—a stool.

We all began to read the funny papers. The bed bell rang and the Major came in to lead us in prayer. She read from the Bible. Some of the girls could talk together on their fingers, clasped behind their backs. The Major talked about the great divine joy of Easter and of motherhood and prayed, asking the deity to forgive us for the great sin we had committed, and be lenient with us, and help us lead better lives in the future. Somebody must have made a mistake about the song because it was "Hark the Herald Angels Sing," which is a Christmas song, but everyone sang as loud as they could because it's a pleasure to sing and everybody sang,

Hark the herald angels sing

Wally Simpson stole our king

and Julia began to giggle so that the Major said, You may go, Julia, and she turned at the door and thumbed her nose at the Major and I felt an awful tickle of laughter like I was going to hoot and howl. Alice pinched me and smiled and pretended she was singing.

We marched upstairs. You could see all our gingham dresses exactly alike. I undressed and got in the gunny sack and big shoes and I could hear somebody crying in their pillow from the next room, and the cries of the hungry babies in the nursery. Alice touched my cheek and showed me a tiny flashlight she had under her pillow. I didn't feel sleepy so we began to "talk."

She wrote, *Don't cry. We, the common people, suffer together.*

I didn't know what she meant. How did she know I felt sad?

She nodded and wrote again, *Nothing can hold us apart. . . . See . . . even deafness,* then she wrote, *or loneliness,* and then, *or fear.*

I wrote, *How?*

117

We are organizing, she wrote.
I read it.
Then she wrote, *Nothing can stop us.*
The matron came down the hall and her face went dark and you couldn't hear a sound. When she had passed, the light went on again and Alice was leaning over the pad.
I read, *I am with the Workers Alliance.*
I looked at it a long time. I wrote, *Amelia too.*
She nodded and smiled.
I chewed the pencil and then I wrote, *I worked all my life.*
She read it and nodded and pointed to herself shaking her head in a quick and joyful way and pointed to her own breast. She grabbed the pad. She looked at me like she loved me then she wrote swiftly.
I took the pad. I was excited. I read, *We are both workers!*
She rolled over, the light went out and I could hear her laughing. I began to laugh too. When she turned on the light again we could not write fast enough.
I wrote, *What does it do, the Workers Alliance?*
They demand food, jobs, she wrote quickly.
I looked at the word *demand.* It was a strong word. I didn't know what to write. I looked at it a long time. She looked at me, and when I looked at her she smiled and nodded, like she was going through woods and I was following her. She leaned over and the light shone through her thin hand. She put her hand under he cheek, closed her eyes which I saw meant sleep, and then she wrote in a bold hand and turned the tiny light on it.
Wake tomorrow!

37

It was Amelia got me out of there before I delivered. After I got out, I almost wished I had stayed in behind those walls. It got very hot in St. Paul that summer. I could hardly walk. I felt like mama. I thought of mama and Butch. I couldn't remember whether I told Butch I kept the baby, or did he hear me? Still, in the daytime I couldn't help but walk proud and seem to smile like some fruit of this summer. I would feel I might die on some lonely night but in the day I felt, like Amelia, that all had the right to live.

Sometimes I couldn't help looking for Butch as if he would get out of the heat in some cool bar. I would go in and pretend to read. People were out in the parks for the cool. I walked up Third in the evening and looked for the Irish star, Oryan Butch always had called it, I didn't know then it was a joke. Butch always said I didn't know a joke when it hit me. I passed the German Village, run by someone else now. Often I tried to look in but the windows only relfected the street and my face. One day I went in and a strange bartender was reading the paper.

I said, I just want to sit down. I'll order something later.

O.K., sister, he said, it is sure hot.

It was cleaner than we kept it. It was very quiet and very clean and I could only see the knuckles of the bartender's hands holding the paper.

I opened my pocketbook and looked in the mirror, and read a leaflet from the Workers Alliance, but I kept thinking—what did Butch want? He was playing the wrong game. They were all trying to win—what? It was the wrong holdup, the wrong home run. It was funny but I kept thinking and feeling like I had just outfoxed the cops, the whole shebang, cracked the vault, made my getaway with the loot under my belly. And I am the Treasure.

What are you laughing about? Amelia said, sitting down beside me— *They just took Clara to give her electric shock treatments. Nothing we could do could stop them. Nothing.*

I never saw her so angry, her face was burning and her little black hat seemed like a fist. O we don't stay at the bottom, covered with slime, shot through with shocks to kill the memory so we won't remember who done it. I am going to get a committee just for you and Clara, you got to have milk.

You'll just make them mad and we won't get anything, I said.

What do you get now? They won't give you anything for love. You got to fight for it. You can't just cry for yourself. You got to cry for all. Some face has got to shine with every other face. We must know that our suffering is together . . . the same enemy after us . . . the same mother over us, she said.

I couldn't say I wouldn't go to the relief office with her. We had to get Clara back before they killed her. The office was packed with a line to my window going outside and down the block in the hot sun. I couldn't lose my place so I stood there my legs swelling. Then there was a kind of shaking of the line, a disturbance up front, and I saw Amelia and an old worker open the door, press past the line and go in. After awhile Amelia backed out the door crying out—Well death doesn't wait either. I tell you a mother needs milk and Clara is dying. I'll get a hundred people back here!

Just before closing time I got up to my caseworker and she said some paper was lost and I had to sign something and they couldn't do anything until they found the paper. I said it was about my time now and I hadn't any milk or iron they said I needed.

We're doing the best we can, she said, come back tomorrow. I began to cry, thinking about Clara. What about Clara, she is supposed to have oranges and milk. Amelia put her arm around me and we left.

We went out and walked up and down the street. Amelia had saved up four nickels from berry picking to buy some milk for Clara. She cried, O Girl the breasts of our mothers are deep with this sorrow, always remember that. We can't tell what happens to us in secret even.

What's there to do? I said.

It'll be buried deep in our class, she said, it will come out. It always comes out.

We walked along the streets. She was a strong walker. She would walk from one end of the city to the other with her leaflets. On Sunday she would walk all day knocking on doors, talking to women. She would walk right in and help them with the baby and show them how to make a meat pie out of leavings, and then she would talk to them and tell them not to believe what was in the papers.

She said, They'll get you sooner or later. They wear you out, they work you to death, they wear you out on the belt, in the mill, the factory. They get your blood and bones one way or another. What are we? Just goods to be bought and sold? Yes, she answered herself cursing, that's what they think, buy and sell you and then use your body after you're dead! It's too bad, it's too bad they can't kill our babies and eat them like suckling pigs. What tender meat that would be! Stuffed babies with mushrooms. Why not?

Everyone will hear, I said. I could hardly keep up with her. I was heavy now.

Let them! she cried, let them! They'll get you soon enough. Everybody might as well know it, the sooner the better. They get you before you got time to learn anything. You don't know what it is about. They stuff you up with fine words and then they stick you in the stomach like a pig.

It got dark. We kept walking around like madwomen. She told me all kinds of stories I never heard before. She said her son was in Centralia and they smacked tar and feathers on him and set fire to him and others and they had to run and it was dark as hell smoke, she said, and they were bleeding and crawling on their knees to a shack, and he couldn't work for a year, and then he was always thinking how he could get a man named Becker out of the pen. Then, she said, when they hung Wesley Everett they hung him by a long rope so *they* could all have souvenirs and you go there, in the best houses, you'll find a piece of that rope, and they are glad to show it to you. That's the kind they are, she said.

I was scared. I never heard this before. And she said, You see the picture I got in my room of the two men, one with a handlebar mustache. I saw it there a lot of times. I thought it was maybe her husband and her father. It's in a big frame with paper roses around it. She said, they were a peddler of fish, and a shoemaker. They were murdered, she said. Sacco and Vanzetti.

Who is doing all that? I said after awhile. Why, they just force a girl on the streets, and Clara having all those abortions and now electric shock treatments that they say will make you forget, and the girl in the home dying having a baby! I used to go around with Clara and where is she now? Who cares if she had a name even, who cares about her blood and bones, who she loved, the way she walked?

I care, Amelia says.

Who else?

All that knew what she knew. All that feel the same, they are together, all with hands like that from working their enduring life. All that are followed and worked to the bone and hounded and bled and murdered.

I knew then I was one of them.

We were standing beneath a great cottonwood tree that leaned green over us like a mother. Yes, she said, putting her hands on my shoulders, a new heart is growing.

38

I'll never forget that summer as long as I live. That big old warehouse where we all lived, five floors, mostly women and it was cool too, with thick brick walls and high windows where sometimes the sun came through like in a temple. There was no heat and no light, and some women who had lived there in the winter had built fires on the wood floors and they had burnt through and made holes, so you could look down or holler down to the floor below. A guy had run electric wires from the outside to the floor we lived on, the second, so we could have lights and an electric plate when nobody was looking. Sometimes cops came, seeing a light, but we had a system of jiggers, it was called, jiggers the cops are coming. It would start at the bottom and go right up through the building.

It was said that it was owned by a widow of the lumber maggots, we called them, and that before the depression when it was rented she went to Europe every summer, but it had been empty now and had been taken over by girls and women who had no place to live.

On the second floor some women had made partitions, a few feet high, and some had hung blankets making a little privacy. Clara had an old mattress there without any springs. Belle in one corner had brought her stuff from above the German Vilage long after Hoinck was buried. I had a pallet on the floor. Amelia had her single cot. She had moved it in after the Workers Alliance offices had been raided and they barely got out with the mimeograph machine, which now sat in the middle of the floor and could be covered with an old oil cloth and boards to put over to make it look like a table. A Jesus lover named Sara, who had lived in the office, came too. Sitting in a rocking chair rocking with her coat and hat on no matter what the weather was Butch's crazy mother. She spooked me out because day and night she talked about Butch and sometimes I thought she knew this was Butch's baby.

She'd kind of grab me and hold me and say, They are playing out in the sand box, honey, Butch and Bill. Maybe you should keep an eye on them. I always had corn fritters for breakfast, she'd say, I make the best corn fritters. I'll make them for supper. Buckwheat cakes and Indian butter makes you fat and a little bit fatter, Butch always says. I keep my own hens. They been laying right good.

She made me turn cold.

It was goofy. Sometimes from all corners would come this singing and these goings on. Belle was trying on black veils to mourn for Hoinck and she would be saying, Yes sir, when Hoinck pawned his tools that was the end of us all. What tools is to a man. He pawned his tools, he pawned more than his tools. He pawned his skill, being able to do something that gives a man pride. What can a man do without tools? He has to lick the boots of crazies like Ganz.

Clara before the shock treatments would be fixing her face, and singing and crying—I'd like to belong to a prominent family. I had my fortune told and there is something good around the corner. I'm going to miss the best pictures. Has "Love in the Tropics" gone away yet? Is it summer yet?

And Sara the Jesus lover would be singing—Jesus, lover of my soul, let me to thy bosom fly.

Belle would howl, lordgodjesus and the virginmary if we all had a bosom to fly to.

Jesus will be waiting for you, Sara would say, Jesus loves you.

Jesus loves you this I know, 'cause the Bible tells me so, Belle would sing.

Sara would bring her Bible to read to us all—In his house are many mansions, if it were not so I would have told you.

Clara would say, I don't think I would need more than fourteen rooms, seven upstairs and seven down and I could have a room of my own.

It was a still hot bright afternoon when they brought Clara back from Hastings Mental Hospital where she had the electric shock treatment and I never seen anything like she looked. It wasn't that she was white, she was always very white, it was that look in her eyes and her stillness. She was very very still as if she had gone out of herself, as if the shock like an explosion had sent the doves of her spirit flying away never to come back.

They were kind of walking her and the social worker who had refused her milk came in behind her and helped her to lie down.

She is going to be just fine, she said to all of us, you'll see. These treatments take away anxiety.

Did you bring the special food she was supposed to get? Amelia asked, going over to stroke Clara's head where it seemed like you could see bruises.

These things take time, the social worker said.

But death don't wait, Amelia said.

Sara began to sing, Shall we gather at the river, the beautiful, beautiful river.

She ought to be living in a better place but this will do till winter, the social worker said, and I hope you will be careful not to have any men up here. You can't get any help if there are goings on with men. You have to be mighty careful.

I waited for Clara to say something awful to her but her eyes seemed to be half closed and her little mouth hung open.

Belle said, O shit.

Amelia said, What about the cod liver oil?

That's the trouble with you people. You are alarmists. Hysterical. I have to fill out this paper. Do you own a truck?

Belle hooted, We ain't got a pot to piss in or a window to throw it out.

Vulgarities will get you nowhere, she said.

Nothing will get us nowhere fast, Belle spat after her as she turned to go and had to walk around the hole burnt in the floor, through which I could see the frightened women gathered down below.

When she left I started to read out loud the paper I had taken while at the relief office, the report on me. I got to the part where it said, The girl is maladjusted, emotionally unstable and a difficult problem to get to talk. A change of environment would be helpful. . . .

Belle hooted, Miami or Pasadena . . . or the Bahamas. . . .

Continuous casework should follow up the birth of the child. Educational interests should be encouraged to get her away from her friend Clara, a prostitute she lives with.

Shhh, Amelia said but Clara didn't hear. I knew already she was far away and it was too late.

I went on—In our opinion there should be a referral to a psychiatrist if she shows symptoms of further emotional and mental disturbance.

Honey, Belle cries, it appears you are upset by something.

I went on reading, She should be tested for sterilization at the birth of her baby. In our opinion sterilization would be advisable.

Amelia was trying to give Clara a drink—It's because they don't need any more children from workers. They don't need us to reproduce our kind.

Belle threw the empty bottle against the wall. It's rotten, stinking, covered with slime! Men after you, the welfare workers after you, people living off each other like rats. I told you I would have no kids to bring into it. Thirteen abortions I had, got 'em out of me.

Butch's mother said, It's wicked, wicked, be careful for the children, that's the future. Where are my children? she suddenly howled like a wolf, my children. I thought they were outside playing in the sand box. It has gotten dark and Butch is gone.

I put my arms around her and rocked the chair and shhhed her.

Sara cried out, Woe! woe! to the Pharisees, Herod is waiting for the little one. Be careful.

Tears were coming out of Clara's eyes and she looked so tiny. She wasn't saying anything or making a face, just tears came out of her eyes and Amelia wiped them away.

It's in the Bible, every man under his own tree. Every worker worthy of his hire to be paid by sundown. Now we see face to face, sisters, Sara said.

Amelia said, We all got to be together. Protect each other. Not lay down or give in. We got to fight for each other.

O maybe it's bad to have a child now, I cried, feeling it leap inside me like a fish in clear water. I put my arms around Clara—Don't cry Clara, we suffer together. We are women. Nothing can hold us apart. I hurt where you hurt. What did they do to your head? Your mouth is bleeding and torn.

Clara's eyes opened in an awful horror. Her little mouth formed a round O but nothing came out. I saw in her eyes a terrible thing.

I gave out a cry. It seemed like the women below gave out a cry and the women above, and Belle screamed.

Clara clung to me and I just rocked her. She was so tiny and smelled like scorch or burn. And the terrible deeps seemed to open up.

39

It was a hot night. Even when Belle threw a whiskey bottle and broke out the tall warehouse windows that you couldn't open. And Amelia said— What about the winter?

The winter, Belle screamed, who's going to be here in the winter?

And I thought for the first time about the winter with a baby, and how mama lost her first baby with the croup the first winter. Where would we be? I thought of going home to mama, and then I thought of Amelia and the Workers Alliance, and I looked at the mimeograph machine sitting in the middle of the floor as if it was some kind of shrouded altar, like they covered the statues in the church, Friday before Easter rising.

I looked at Clara who had not moved in the night, and Butch's mother asleep in the rocking chair, who never took off her hat, waiting to go find Butch.

Amelia got up very early and took up her black hat and her bag of leaflets and went out, tiptoeing so as not to wake anyone. The demonstration for the fresh milk was at noon. I wasn't going to tell her about the little pains I had had all night, still about an hour apart. It was surely time now. Butch, I said into the hot still air, you always said, it's the timing. That was about robbing a bank, making a homer, ringing the bell, bringing home the bacon. But women know the most about that. When you're going to have a baby there is some kind of strange timing. You can't wait for appropriations, or the social worker to sign the ambulance paper!

I began to think anyway how I would call the ambulance, if no one had a nickel or a dime. I didn't even have a watch to time the pains. I could count seconds, count one was a second, sixty made a minute. Belle must have some cash stashed away somewhere. Belle was sleeping amongst empty bottles with the newspaper clipping on Hoinck's death clutched in her hand. Her purse was under her pillow. In a little sewing box on the floor I found two pennies. I decided to wait till she woke.

The woman from downstairs stood at the big open door. It was so high it made people look small. It was not for people. I did not know her name. I knew she walked miles with Amelia, passing out leaflets.

I came for the leaflets, she said, and she lifted up her top skirt and inside she had like aprons with pockets. My husband is a hard shell, she said, so I got these little pockets. I put the leaflets in here.

I wanted to ask her if she had a baby and how it was. Why hadn't I asked mama. O, if she was only here.

I got to jump a wink ahead of my husband, she said, putting the leaflets in all the pockets. Amelia called up through the hole, Ho there, we got to get along. Pass these out downtown before the milk demonstration.

Coming! coming! the woman said, I thought joyfully. I wished I was going too. I saw Clara was groaning kind of, and moving her hand up as if trying to wipe something away from her head. I ran over to her and took her hand which was real cold and clammy. I began to rub her and she pulled away like she was frightened.

It's me, it's me, I said, and she opened her bloodshot eyes. Her eyes were terrible, the whites bloody, and the pupils as if leaping right out of the sockets to tell you something. I remember the lovely eyes of Clara so full of summer flowers. Someone had taken her far away and I wanted to bring her back, let her tell me about the fourteen-room house and the sunken baths and a room of her own.

Clara! Clara! I cried—remember me, remember how you took me on your wanderings, how you showed me everything.

She didn't even smile. Those pupils leapt out though, as if to tell me something terrible. They told me. I saw it all, what they had done to her.

Clara! remember the German Vilage and those Saturday nights with the Booya and Bill, I cried, Bill and Butch, those pretty fellows, those wonderful foxes you used to call them, those slick cats you said. . . . Remember?

Was there a flicker, a kind of wink? One eye kind of closed and then opened. I felt I mustn't let her forget. They can't do that to her. I lifted up her cold thin body and her head rolled and it looked like her hair was greasy and bruises on the temples. What had they done?

I held her, I shook her, I caressed her, I shouted at her. Butch's mother woke and watched us. Sara sat up and wound her hair. Even Belle stirred.

Memory is all we got, I cried, we got to remember. We got to remember everything. It is the glory, Amelia said, the glory. We got to remember to be able to fight. Got to write down the names. Make a list. Nobody can be forgotten. They know if we don't remember we can't point them out. They got their guilt wiped out. The last thing they take is memory. Remember, Amelia says, the breasts of your mothers. O mama help us now. Clara remember your mama like you told me, going from city to city, to lousy jobs and getting children and taking them on her back, and locking them in rooms while she waited on tables, did laundry, Clara you got to remember your mama, I'll help you.

Then she smiled and the pupils changed kindly and she said—Baby. I grabbed my belly, Yes Clara, remember how you stood on the cold street to get enough money to help me. Yes, Clara, a baby. Remember, you want to see it. A pang went through me like a quake. I wasn't counting now. You're gonna hold it, I said. Yes you will see it, you remember the baby, see they can't wipe it out. Nothing can wipe it out. Remember that, Clara, we'll remember for you. We'll help you bit by bit, all of it, all our great lousy beautiful and terrible life, you'll see, we'll remember it all, all. I remember every insult those rich johns gave you that night, Clara, and you shining like a light, that's what you are a light, Clara, a prairie city light. Don't forget it!

Sara came over and took hold of my shoulders and laid Clara down but her face was not so pale now, and her eyes followed me, and she said clearly but slowly, Clara, Clara, name the baby, she said, means Clear Light, the baby. Clara!

Yes, yes, I cried, Claro clara cleara light yes . . .

Sara walked me slowly away saying, What shall we do, our little sister has no breasts. . . .

O, a breast for all, I cried, and milk for all. . . .

Yes! yes! Sara said, she felt so tall and kind with an odor of strange love coming from her widow's weeds, her straight body like something defending, protecting you. . . . Butch's mother rose, with a strange knowing as if she recognized me at last and she bowed and touched me and helped me into her rocking chair.

Butch is working just outside there on the street, she said, I can see him through the window. He'll come in for lunch. Butch, she cried softly, your girl is going to have corn fritters with us for lunch.

I bent over with a sudden pain and Belle cried, Is it starting? Holy Moses, I bet this is going to be some kid. I feel funny, I'm wet as a drowned cat, remember Susybelly? Say, did you get the signed paper for the ambulance. Say, you got to call them. Anybody got a nickel? Here in my sewing basket . . .

I took the two cents already, I said, but pennies aren't any good. You got to have the nickel for Ma Bell.

Somebody must have a nickel. Is it possible nobody has a nickel? Yes, it is possible. It is certainly possible. Cash scarce as hens' teeth. Hoinck's old suit, maybe some cash. I put money in old shoes too. I was going to buy some diapers.

I began to count the seconds, putting a finger up for each sixty making a minute. The next one came at eight minutes.

I felt good.

I thought of my life with Butch. It makes you shake to come from your own loneliness and death. It makes you shake all over, but you've got to do it, you've got to take the chance to do it. It takes guts to speak out of the lonely room, after looking at yourself in a mirror, after smelling out yourself alone, after hearing emptiness sound off. It makes the sweat stand on you, and your blood starts up, for what is one voice alone, or what good is it to cry in a room with the door shut?

The pains got worse so I couldn't walk. Belle was making coffee and I sat down and looked at the clock. Now it was six minutes apart. It was exciting. I wanted to see it right away. Maybe it would look like Butch, with a lean black head and a sharp face. I could feel my blood like a river inside me, and my breast deep and thigh and womb ready for a new child, and strong labor for it and I liked it. I remember Amelia said once, I tell you when I like it, when there is something to it, when there's something doing, when you can see it, put your face in it, and double up your fist for it. That's when I like it, she said.

I had my teeth in it now for the first time. I could feel it bear down, bear heavy.

I'll go out on the street, Belle said, I'll phone. You got everything ready, kid?

I'm ready, I said.

Ain't you gonna take anything? Belle said.

I got nothing to take, I said, this tie of Butch's. The two cents. She can start to college on that.

Say kid, be careful, what about your income tax? I'll bring you a Dr. Pepper.

I'll need a doctor, I said and she hooted with laughter, and I could hear her with her wonderful heavy step going downstairs.

It was then I heard Clara, such a little gasp was her last. I knew it right away. Clara, I cried, Clara don't go.

I got her little mirror from her purse, where she always looked at herself, I held it up to her mouth which was now in an awful O shape as if her last breath hurt.

The mirror was empty.

40

I was glad to close her eyes over the horror they had given her and shut her silent screaming mouth. Butch's mother held the bucket while we washed her and brushed her golden hair. She was like a bird is when the life goes out of them, they seem so tiny, just bones and feathers. Amelia would say it was how a body got without proper food and being cold all winter and somebody after her.

Sara took from her things a white dress like a bride's with lace. We would make it cling and it had a high neck that covered the bruises, and Sara was saying something from the Bible, like—Set me as a seal upon thy heart, for love is stronger than death . . . many waters cannot quench love, neither can the floods drown it. We have a little sister and she has no breasts. What shall we do for our sister in the day when she shall be spoken for? If she be a wall we will build upon her a palace of silver and if she be a door we will enclose her with cedar. She made some sign upon her and her voice was low. Make haste, she said above her, be thou like a roe or a young deer upon the mountains of spices.

Butch's mother put a cloth rose between her hands.

I didn't need to count the pains now. I didn't worry about them, or the ambulance. And it wasn't long before it seemed all the people from the demonstration came, kind of anxious and hurrying, into the big room now full of noon sun—all the street girls and the sewing women from the project, and Amelia her face flushed and her hat gone, and when she knelt beside Clara the other women knelt too and each one was singing or saying whatever song or prayer she knew and some sobbed and cried out.

Belle came to me. How is it, kid? I called the ambulance but they seemed like they never heard of you, didn't get the requisition or whatever the hell it is. Kid you should have seen the demonstration, hundreds outside the courthouse and the cops threw tear gas out the windows and some of those ballplayers caught the bombs and threw them right back and kid, you should have seen those bureaucrats, like rats, pouring out of the building, and the street littered with those leaflets saying Milk and Iron Pills for Clara.

There was a big line going out into the hot noon sun and the cops were lined up across the street, but not one dared to come in. Pretty soon around Clara were gifts, like lipstick, old paper flowers, chains and medallions of the Virgin Mary, ribbons, belts, little pictures of saints. It looked like whatever a person had, they put there for Clara. Some combed her hair, patted her pretty dress, said a prayer, and some sang little songs for her.

I couldn't get over it, that they should all care, as Amelia says, a breast for all—the men kind of hung back but the women gathered and I tell you with the sun pouring down as if free for all, I never in my life saw anything like it. I felt I would stand there and just drop my child into their hands, the Great Mothers, that's what I saw and will always see as long as I draw breath. I got no words but it will be like I had told Clara, inside us forever. Remembering always and appearing in everything, great mirrors like we held the picture of all, the suffering of all. I saw mama there, the same bend of back, the sagging belly, the look of sorrow, and of something else, something fierce, and the reason you have a child maybe.

Amelia held up her hands—Listen. Attention please, she said.

Sara said, We must have a mass for Clara.

Amelia said—Yes a memorial for Clara, a mass meeting, let our voice be heard in the whole city—a trial, a judgment against the city fathers, a trial yes, an accusation. We accuse. Yes, we point a finger. We hold them responsible.

There was a kind of roar that went down the stairs and out into the street as it was passed down from one person to another.

When? Tomorrow? The next day. Everyone seemed to agree on everything. Yes. Take it down, Sara. We have a good stencil left. Take all suggestions down, Amelia said, everything. All accusations. People called out. Clara is dead. Who killed Clara? Why didn't she have milk and iron pills? Who didn't care if she died? Who doesn't care that we are hungry? Some would begin to tell what had happened to them in the relief office but it would go on, everyone crying out something. I helped take down the ideas.

Was she a criminal? Was she a danger? Clara never got any wealth. She died a pauper. She never stole timber or wheat or made poor flour. She never stole anyone's land or took it for high interest on the mortgage. She never got rich on the labor of others. She never fattened off a war. She never made ammunition or guns. She never hurt no one. Who killed Clara? *Who will kill us?*

O it was something to hear and see their anger. And their power. Amelia looked like the mother of them all, nodding, smiling.

Did you get that? Put that down.

Sara said, Amen.

Amelia said, Go, Sara, and get that on the stencil. You can use the typewriter at the Labor Temple. They'll let you. Come back here as soon as you can. O yes, get some paper from them. Tell them about Clara and the Girl. They'll give it.

They kept coming and coming, a steady line. Belle made me lie down on her bed. Amelia said she had delivered a hundred babies and would deliver a hundred more.

They made a little cave in the corner. Amelia rubbed me. Belle was crying and holding my hand. Then I saw Butch's mother and I touched her and she knew everything. And I thought of Butch and how he thought it was all a ball game. It ain't a ball game, honey, I was laughing.

O it's shit to have to lie on the floor, Belle said.

Now breathe, Amelia said, bear down—breathe—bear down—breathe—

O Butch, I laughed, you didn't know what your mama knew, that little woman, door to you all. How did you do it? I asked her. As she giggled, a high whinny, I saw her eye was like Butch's eye. I reached for her, put my arms around her, and she lay against me like a little wren, crying in that high voice.

It's the realest dream. I saw Amelia leaning between my legs looking at me saying, breathe—push—wait—breathe. It was like being run over by a truck when the pains came. But the women were pressing around now, I could look into their faces. They seem to breathe with me, a kind of great wind through their bodies like wind in a woods. Amelia said she delivered many babies and would many more. She kept talking. I didn't hear her and it was funny it was like when I left Butch on the prairie covering him with a blanket and his breath gone.

Breathe, Amelia kept saying, wait—push—stop—breathe—

He asked me before he died, Do we belong to the human race? Some people think we don't, I told him, but we do. Yes we do. This is your face, Butch, coming back down the great river, the great dark. I was bucking like a goat, lifting like a mountain. I heard the mimeograph start. A kind of beat.

It's crowning, Amelia cried, I never had heard that. The crown of its head. It's all right, just turn the head. Now, easy and strong Girl, O Girl it's coming, easy now. I felt all the river broke in me and poured and gave and opened. Was it my cry, the cry of the women, the cry of a child? The last breath of Butch, the first of a child. Covered with a kind of slime and dark she lay the child on me. A girl, she cried, a girl, and she rubbed the slime and the child let a little gasp and breathed and before my eyes turned and glowed the dark memory, flushing. She turned golden as Clara, even her wet hair.

Belle was shouting, It's a girl, and the women murmured happily, It's a girl!

A woman, Amelia cried, still wiping the body with her hands.

Belle was shouting, and for a moment the mimeiograph stopped then began again.

It's a woman, Belle was shouting, a sister a daughter. No dingle dangle, no rod of Satan, no sword no third arm, a girl a woman a mother.

Amelia cried, Ho ho, a new woman.

Light, I said, Claro Clara.

Her name is Clara, the women said, a kind of woman's humming was all around me. I saw mama in them all, the bearing the suffering in us all, their seized bodies, bent bellies hanging, and the ferocity of their guarding. I felt fierce and she seemed to burrow to the nipple as I saw Amelia take the knife she had soaking in alcohol in a beer bottle and cut the cord.

Then Butch's mother said quite clearly, You keep the cord and then when the child is lost and wandering they come back to the grandmothers to find their road, the cord will tell them the road. The road.

I saw the women pressing in to see and I held her up for all to see and heard a kind of sound like AHHHHHHHHH of wonder and delight.

Amelia said, Give me a newspaper to put the afterbirth in. And Butch's mother became very excited, Give it to me, she said, give it to me. Amelia wrapped it and gave it to her. They say, she said, it has more protein in it than any living thing.

Now I could cup her tiny bright head. I cried out. She had the tiny face of my mother. Like in a mirror.

O girl, I said down to her, giving her my full breast of milk.

Afterwords

This memorial to the great and heroic women of the depression was really written by them. As part of our desperate struggle to be alive and human we pooled our memories, experiences and in the midst of disaster told each other our stories or wrote them down. We had a writers' group of women in the Workers Alliance and we met every night to raise our miserable circumstances to the level of sagas, poetry, cry-outs.

There was no tape recorder then so I took their stories down. Some could not write very well, and some wrote them out painfully in longhand while trying to keep warm in bus stations or waiting for food orders at relief offices.

They looked upon me as a woman who wrote (like the old letter writers) and who strangely and wonderfully insisted that their lives were not defeated, trashed, defenseless but that we as woman contained the real and only seed, and were the granary of the people. This should be the function of the so-called writer, to mirror back the beauty of the people, to urge and nourish their vital expression and their social vision.

The family of the Girl is the family of Gladys who wrote it all out of her agony and there was enough for a book. Where is it now? The getting and birthing of the child is the story of Natalie, who has been for thirty years or more in an asylum and is still alive. She also has a story for a book. Butch's death soliloquy a girl wrote down from remembering leaving her lover like that after a bootleg shootout. The bank robbery was reported by the girl who drove the car. Belle and Hoinck—and these were their names—ran a German Village on St. Peter Street. I never could get Belle to tell her terrible story entirely. She was ashamed.

So the publishing of this book is wonderful—to be made visible now by a new generation, not born yet when these women sent them a message—a hosanna, a shout of joy and strength back to those wonderful women our mothers ourselves who keep us all alive.

Meridel Le Sueur
St. Paul, Minnesota
October 1978

This is a story of our mothers. It tells us something about ourselves. It is also the window through which we can see our grandmothers and great-grandmothers. We can get the dates, places and the roles of government by reading old newspapers and history books. But we will not find out how our mothers survived there. They are not mentioned.

When we can see how our mothers survived, we can see our own survival. And we can make choices for ourselves. We can even decide who is at fault.

Stories of poverty always make those who are affluent feel sorry for the poor. But this story makes you respect those who gathered together to grow, to help one another and to bring life into what seemed to be a life-less world. If they had not offered this to us we would not be here. What greater respect can one have than to recognize that?

It is not only important to remember but it is as important to tell our own stories. *The Girl* brings the strength to honor the struggles of our mothers . . . and, therefore, to honor our own struggles . . . and to pass them to our daughters. Without the knowledge of her reality, how can a woman decide her own life? Her mother's life is part of her reality. It must not be denied.

Rachel Tilsen
St. Paul, Minnesota

I can still hear my own grandmother calling me "Girl." It was a word of promise and love, a word that rolled richly from her heart, a special word for the young, still-learning child-woman. She never prefaced it with "lit-tle"—that came mostly from other adults in my life—adults anxious to prove their superiority. She called me "Girl," and it was our secret word for a very special place in the world.

This special kind of girl is the dominant rhythm in Meridel Le Sueur's *The Girl*. Here is a young girl, half formed but learning. A girl learning quickly from the life around her, a girl growing strong in her struggle to-ward womanhood and a place in the culture of the people. I hesitate to call her the "heroine" of the story, for Meridel's sensitive and brilliant portrayal of this young woman cannot be so narrowly circumscribed. The girl is much more. She is the girl in all of us, the kernel of our humanity.

The story takes us back to the thirties and a culture of poverty and oppression. Truer, deeper rhythms of that experience have seldom sur-faced. In *The Girl*, Meridel gives us an extraordinary historical document of how people actually *felt*, and how they lived and survived those dark years. While many writers during the thirties "took to the road" to "find' the American experience of the Depression, Meridel Le Sueur, like most other people, had stayed put, and in staying with her people and her neighbors, recorded a unique, and perhaps the truest, story of her times.

Meridel does not tell us about the thirties—she invites us to join in that experience. She takes us into a darkened movie theater and opens the panorama of the thirties for us to see the rhythms of that culture, those people. It is a stark world, different from the flowering prairies of the Midwestern farms and villages. Its rhythms are not of the movement of grasses, but of the wrenching movements of urban poverty and the be-ginnings of our modern bureaucratic world.

But it is from the culture of women that the hungry young girl seeks the way to growth and maturity. And it is from this source, stylistically, that *The Girl* is so unique and powerful. The story is not so much a "plot" as it is a pattern—a pattern reflecting the underlying spirit of a truly revo-lutionary human culture. Meridel's words and rhythms move us into a vibrant awareness of the underlying forces of our collective experiences. She renders in bold strokes not the "representation" of reality, but a poignant and intense reality of the human personality. Like the "new" music, *The Girl* resonates to more basic rhythms. This is not "slice of life," photographic realism, but an inner realism of human strength and growth.

You will come to "know" the story and the characters not because you are manipulated, or led, or forced, but because you will make the connections at a more subtle level—the level of love and solidarity.

Like any true work of art, this work focuses on process. Fused into an organic whole, we become involved in the experience itself, the unfolding of that place in the personal and cultural history of all of us. *The Girl* will become part of our lives, our experiences. It will come back to haunt and possess us, to enchant us, to include us in the great human struggle!

Dr. Neala Schleuning
Mankato, Minnesota

Looking at the garden I created over twenty years ago, plants grown so interwined and complex, I felt overwhelmed by it and longed to see the garden I had planted in its simpler, original state. I hired a young man to help me clear out the underbrush and prune and clip and pull and tear until I could recognize at least the outlines of what I had put into the earth so long ago. Plants are like people. They grow in so many directions that you can't recognize them after they have weathered too many seasons. But to my delight and surprise, when the intertwining ivy, the laurel and mirror plant was removed from a certain corner of the garden, there stood a camelia in the exact shape, form and size that I had planted it twenty years ago! I greeted it with the delight of recognition.

I had somewhat the same feeling on reading Meridel's novel, *The Girl*, written in 1939! That was almost forty years ago. I have known Meridel for forty years and have seen her complex mind grow ever more complex. She has become as abundant, incredibly rich, composted and intertwined as my garden, and her writing style too reflects her complexity and her vigorous, unpruned growth. After all, since 1939 we have known the Second World War, Hitler's "Final Solution," the hydrogen bomb, the McCarthy repression, the Korean War, the assassinations, the moon walks, and finally that obscene shock to our humanity, the Vietnam War. Who of us has remained the same?

But here is *The Girl*. Like my camelia. Just as Meridel planted it in 1939 when so many of us were on fire with the dream of a "bright new world" in the midst of the worst depression in history—as Meridel puts it, "more terrible than a war." We battled it with organization. The Workers Alliance for the unemployed; the C.I.O. unions for the underpaid and the overworked. And peace organizations in the shadow of the coming holocaust.

As I read this book I felt an abysmal sorrow that after forty years these characters and these problems should still be recognizable. In fact, compared to the poverty of today, with 60 percent of young Blacks and Chicanos unemployed in the midst of galloping inflation and conspicuous consumption, the poverty of 1939 seems almost tame. Certainly the violence and desperation seem understated compared to the violent and alienated world we live in now. Meridel herself in another story gives the reason: "Capitalism is a world of ruins really, junk piles of machines, men, women, bowls of dust, floods, erosions, masks to cover rapacity and in this sling and wound the people carry their young, in the shades of their grief, in the thin shadow of their hunger, hope and crop in their hands, in the dark of the machine, only they have the future in their hands. Only they."

In 1978 what gives me as one individual hope is the very fact that such people as Meridel exist to grace the human race. And the fact that the young have rediscovered her, come upon her willy nilly like an oasis in the great Sahara; that they are drinking deeply the fresh water of her humanity and her wisdom, and are renewing themselves to carry on the task which we worked at with so much energy and hope for so long, yet have hardly begun.

Irene Paull
San Francisco, California

Essays

THE BOOK'S PROGRESS: The Making of *The Girl*

by John F. Crawford

I.

I started West End Press in 1976 while I was living in Cambridge, Massachusetts. My object was to print works by American writers neglected by publishers in the "mainstream." In particular, I was interested in young working-class writers, people of color, women, and blacklisted Communist writers of an earlier time. Soon I discovered several stories by the proletarian writer of the thirties, Meridel Le Sueur, in the anthology *Writers in Revolt* (Westbury: Lawrence Hill, 1973). I learned that Meridel was still alive, acquired her address and went to visit her, traveling from New York by Greyhound bus to St. Paul, Minnesota, in January 1977.

I went through her basement, where her manuscripts were stored, and found sufficient materials for what was to become six volumes of her work which I would publish myself: two volumes of short stories, *Harvest* and *Song for My Time* (published later in 1977); two pamphlets, *Women on the Breadlines* (published in 1977) and *Worker Writers* (edited and published in 1982); another pair of longer stories ("The Bird" and "The Horse," published as a part of the volume *I Hear Men Talking* in 1983); and a novel completed in 1939, *The Girl* (published at the end of 1978). Since Feminist Press already had plans to publish a collection of Meridel's work, I had to work around their choices to some degree (they finally published their collection as *Ripening* in 1982). I left a letter with Meridel, dated 1-10-77, promising to begin editing the manuscripts for West End Press. My total operating budget at the time was under $6,000.

Soon after my visit, Meridel wrote a note of appreciation, in which she also remembered the other young people who had recently made a film based on her writings, entitled *My People Are My Home*:

> *I spent all night walking under the pear tree thinking about this . . . I have to express it feebly, poorly, but it is very important, a miracle. . . . This has to do with the reprinting of my literary tracks, pollination out of the primordial mud . . . out of social darkness and struggles and individual annihilations and resurrections [. . .] you all come so sturdily and silently and tenderly to the ruins . . . to the cry, to the silence . . . like loving archaeologists preserving every shard . . . putting all the pieces together as I've seen [done] with jars . . . but rarely with people.*

Deeper in this letter, Meridel added some indication of how she would go about preparing her works for publication—including their revision:

> *I feel my work has all kinds of smog and fog over it: seductions, ambiguities. . . . Some were social and some were sexual . . . perhaps we can show this struggle . . . like from the romantic lyrical personal . . . to the*

137

larger . . . the effect of male structure of writing etc. . . . . It has something to do with the Indian spherical concept when you celebrate winter summer is inside and winter inside summer so you know the turn and re turn. Generations should be like this in true love . . . one generation curled within the other and love and respect for both, and resurrection . . . this is the only resurrection . . . transformation, dialectical transformation.

When I say this indicates "how she would go about . . . revision" you must think I am off the mark—surely this is a whole world view, not a plan for editing books. But this is precisely it; with Meridel, *all* revisions are global, in the sense that they involve the entire universe with regard to its operations on a particular moment.

It remains to be shown *how* the point Meridel raises, "the clearing up of ambiguities," the exposure of a male structure of writing, and the discovery of an "Indian spherical concept" which is also "dialectical transformation" all find their way into such a project.

II.

My preliminary notes on *The Girl* are embarrassingly slight. They read, in total, "Novel of gangsterism. Brilliant scenes with bad connecting links at times. Needs help in editing." More elaborate editing notes, sent to Meridel, suggest cuts in scenes that are either redundant or contradictory, cuts in several chapters which are episodic events outside the main line of action, and many small adjustments, especially links between chapters.

Meridel set about the actual revision process in the fall of 1977. From the beginning, she focused more on her overall intention for the book than on the small structural changes I was looking for. Specifically, she raised four points. She wanted to write an afterword ("to put in some evocation of the women who wrote the story, to give [the] feeling that I recorded it"); she wanted to rework the opening chapters; she wanted to cut some of the "gangster" material; and she was nervous about the conclusion ("What about the end, the very end, do you think that is adequate . . . you can't do too much but is the birth too fast?"). I have a gap in correspondence between these comments and ones she made later, at the end of her revision. In a letter dated January 25, 1978, she remarked with seeming diffidence:

Also I am mailing The Girl *on the weekend. I have got fond of her and the book. I have put some deeper things in it, the beginning is thrilling, and I have deepened the sexual perception of the girls and women. Also the end . . . with all the women much more social and collective I think, and the boy has turned into a girl.*

Meridel warned me in the same letter that technically the manuscript was "quite ragged," that she was working on a "little tiny typewriter which doesn't improve my spelling or spacing," and that she worried that "any of the so-called plot [might be] cut out etc." What she did not say, but was in the back of her mind, was that she was glad to finish the book with her thought processes clear. She had suffered a minor stroke two months before, around Thanksgiving, in St. Paul, giving herself, her family and friends, and I must say her publisher, cause for concern.

There were still the purely structural matters concerning plot which needed fixing. Meridel has always been more interested in what she once called, quoting Joyce, "the curve of emotion" than in the niceties of plotting. The result was, for instance, that in the first draft version of *The Girl* Butch's brother Bill dies twice, at different times in the book, by different means. Here I wish to summarize the major changes Meridel made in the book before we published it in December 1978.

THE AFTERWORD

True to her word, Meridel added an afterword, which gave thanks to "the great and heroic women of the depression," saying that the book was "really written by them." In a memorable passage, she described herself as a scribe recording the words of real women huddled together in a cold building in St. Paul:

> *As part of our desperate struggle to be alive and human we pooled our memories, experiences and in the midst of disaster told each other our stories or wrote them down. We had a writers' group of women in the Workers Alliance and we met every night to raise our miserable circumstances to the level of sagas, poetry, cry-outs. There was no tape recorder then so I took their stories down.* (133)

FRONT MATTER

She kept a dedication to her companion of the period ("To Robert Aaron Brown and that dark city of St. Paul") and to the women who she said wrote the book ("And for Natalie, Anna, Bernice, Gladys, Doris, Sara, all living, all real, all in need"), but cut the motto "Women shall be terrible in story" from Euripides. She added a passage which she had adapted from the Book of Jeremiah, ending, "The land is desolated because of the presence of the oppressor. For the hurt of the daughters of my people, I am hurt." At the last minute, she added to her afterword that this book was made available now to "a new generation, not born yet when these women sent them a message." Subtly in these choices, she affirmed the role of women as continuers of the struggle, rather than as mysterious and terrible oracles, once upon the scene and then gone.

OTHER AFTERWORDS

Meridel encouraged me to solicit three other afterwords, by her daughter Rachel, by university professor Neala Schleuning, and by her friend and Communist party comrade of the thirties Irene Paull. Rachel's note stressed the continuity from mother to daughter, Neala's addressed Meridel's difference as a woman writer, and Irene's recalled the revolutionary promise of the past which was still unfulfilled today. Meridel herself insisted that I *not* cut a passage of Neala's note which remarked of Meridel:

> She renders in bold strokes not the *"representation"* of reality, but a poignant and intense reality of the human personality. Like the *"new"* music, The Girl resonates to more basic rhythms. This is not *"slice of life,"* photographic realism, but an inner realism of human strength and growth. (135)

OPENING SECTION: THE TAVERN

Meridel rewrote extensively the opening section of the novel, creating nine short chapters out of the original six and moving several major incidents, about the Girl's father and family life and about the murder of Butch's brother Bill, back and ahead respectively to gain greater dramatic tension. She brought up to chapter 2 a scene in which Amelia, the Communist organizer in the book, attends the birthing of Susybelly, the cat that belongs to Belle, the owner of the German Village Tavern where the Girl works. (In the original scene, the cat is helped by a "thin man," another Communist, who never returns to the story.) The revised beginning is far more dramatically rendered, full of the action at the German Village (a real, historical tavern in the Rice Park section of old St. Paul), with sharper distinctions among the principal characters arising through dialogue.

An example of this rewriting comes in the scene of the birthing of Susybelly. Butch, the young tough who is about to become the Girl's lover, comments about Susybelly and Amelia answers:

> Boy, Butch said, she got it down machine gun. She can count. Three four five, he counted laughing.
> She's a female like us, Amelia said, she don't know the father, she gives all she's got to make them come out whole healthy full of seed. Hold the light over closer. (6)

By introducing Amelia as a midwife in an early chapter, Le Sueur integrated her into the working-class population of the tavern, gave her an earthy female identity in contrast to the stereotype of the detached and cold "political" organizer, and foreshadowed the end of the book where the surviving women—including Amelia—make common cause in an abandoned building.

MIDDLE SECTION: THE GANGSTER STORY

The next significant changes come at the beginning of what is now chapter 14 (pp. 45 ff.), when the sexual relationship between the Girl and Butch is consummated. Both the Girl's first night with Butch (her first time) and her reflections on her friend Clara's casual prostitution are rendered in a sharper and clearer language than the author had felt was possible in 1939. Beyond that, the language of gender distinction is sharpened. Watching Butch leave the shabby hotel where they have taken a room, the Girl wonders:

> *Had Butch won, struck a foul, thrown a home run, made the bases or struck out? How could you even know? Who would tell you, or say anything, or maybe laugh?* (47)

When she returns to the tavern, she is greeted not just by Clara as in the first version, but by the assembled women:

> *I knew Belle when she came toward me, and I buried my face in the great beery breasts and she lifted my face and looked into it and said, Here baby, sit down, you look like a ghost. Butch's mother stopped and wiped her eyes and Amelia cried, O Girl I am glad to see you, as if I had returned from a kidnapping.* (47)

Clara's response to the news that the Girl is in love with Butch, planning to marry him and buy a service station, is quite different in the second version from the first. In the first she says "Gee that's bad. It'll come to no good," but immediately reverses herself: "Say ain't love wonderful!" In the second version, she is more thoughtful:

> *O kid, that's bad, you're in trouble if you love a guy. He can do anything to you and he will. It seems like they love you at first but they don't, they only want to put it in you. They make out they care for you but O baby, they don't. They'll do you in hell, beat you up, mow you down. O baby, be careful. . . .* (49)

A chapter portraying Clara's own childhood and subsequent life as a sexual victim is dropped; instead Le Sueur ends another chapter—where the Girl waits for Clara to return from the street—with a more philosophical and global comment than is to be found in the first version: "We are growing, in a field that is cold, bitter, sour, and no chance for life" (52).

The whole rewriting of the Girl's discovery of heterosexual love is from the woman's side, with chances for the principal female characters to intervene and affect the Girl's developing consciousness.

In a letter during the revision process, Meridel remarked of Ganz, the gangster who bullies the desperately poor men of the German Village into attempting a bank robbery, that he was "getting [more] obnoxious." It is true: Ganz takes on a more aggressive character, overtly demanding of Butch that the Girl be "nice" to him in exchange for his selection of Butch to join the bank robbers. Butch acquiesces, selling his own girlfriend into prostitution with the gangster by his silence. The Girl acquiesces too, on the strength of a bribe from Ganz. As the men plot the robbery, Ganz moves in on the Girl. The actual act of sex is not portrayed in either the first or second version; Ganz knocks the Girl out first, in the hotel room where they go with a gangster friend of his. When she wakes up, he continues to drill her on her role in the robbery, as if nothing had happened.

The Girl returns to find Butch about to go out with the other men for a "dry run" of the robbery. She stands with Belle watching the men leave.

In the second version, a comment is added which establishes the common perception of the women about the men:

> *It was awful to see the four of them like drowning men from a rotten ship slanting out together, each one alone but in some terrible violence hanging together.* (67)

The actual bank robbery sequence, starting with Butch's and the Girl's last night together in a hotel and ending with the death of the mortally wounded Butch after the Girl drives him away from the failed holdup scene in the getaway car, is unchanged is except for two key additions. In both versions, Butch, drunk before the robbery, has discovered that the Girl is pregnant and tries to persuade her to see an abortionist. But in the second version she actually fools Butch, going to the shack by the river but running out the door again. Also in the second version, on her last night with Butch, a few lines are added in which the Girl, conscious of having deceived Butch about going to the abortionist, looks to the future:

> *And then I felt good. On my own I had done it. I wouldn't tell him until after it was over. I had to smile. I had already robbed the bank. I had stolen the seed. I had it on deposit. It was cached. It was safe.*
> *I had to laugh. It was in a safe. I had the key.* (76)

The revisions of the middle section serve to foreground the community of women, show Ganz and his gangsterism in greater detail, portray Clara the whore as a product of both her choices and her environment, and reveal the Girl holding the "key," the unborn child, in defiance of Butch's orders. All the portrayals of character are more dynamic and reflect to a greater degree what Schleuning called "an inner realism of human strength and growth."

THE END: "THE BOY HAS TURNED INTO A GIRL"

After the death of Butch and the failure of the bank robbery, the Girl returns to St. Paul and rejoins the women, who have taken up residency in a tenement building to fend for themselves without the men. As she comes nearer to term and as Clara, ill from tuberculosis and slow starvation, becomes weaker, the women gather in a tighter bond, and Amelia, the Communist, brings them within the fold of the Workers Alliance.

The beginning of chapter 37 marks another departure from the original text. Three chapters are condensed into two, the death of Clara is postponed to the end of the book, and Amelia is shown actively fighting to save her from the hospital where she is being given electroshock treatments. Part of the "conversion scene," typical of proletarian novels of the thirties, is rewritten; now an impassioned Amelia confronts an equally impassioned Girl over Clara's tragedy. In the second version, the Girl says (changes in roman):

> Who is doing all that? . . . Why, they just force a girl on the streets,

and Clara having all those abortions and now electric shock treatments that they say will make you forget, and the girl in the home
dying having a baby! I used to go around with Clara and where is
she now? *Who cares if she had a name even, who cares about her blood
and bones, who she loved, the way she walked?*

I care, Amelia says.

Who else?

*All that knew what she knew. All that feel the same, they are to-
gether.* All with hands like that from working their enduring life.
All that are followed and worked to the bone and hounded and
bled and murdered.

I knew then I was one of them.

We were standing beneath a great cottonwood tree that leaned
green over us like a mother. Yes, she said, putting her hands on my
shoulders, a new heart is growing. (121)

Cut is a speech by Amelia in the first version, on her own Communist
virtue:

> *She said, A new heart is growing, lubchick. You have to give your life,
> your heart. You have to have a living heart in you, a feeling for all. O
> we must take delight in each other. Be a star. If I see in the paper, she says,
> that a woman in Spain has lost everything, and I see her standing by a
> tub of water in her ruined house I know the same thing she does. She is
> me standing here. All are near to us now. A new heart is growing.*

Amelia is not stripped of her authority in the second version; she is as
much the Communist activist as ever. But she is much more clearly what
the Italian Communist theoretician Gramsci calls the "organic intellectual,"
the activist whose heart is with the people, and she is also all woman, al-
lied with the birth process and attuned to the Girl's reality.

The last chapter of the original is expanded, in a total rewrite, to three
chapters. In the original, the women try frantically to call an ambulance
when the Girl's time has come, but Amelia, returning from a protest meeting over Clara's death, has to deliver the baby herself. The entire birth
scene comprises a short passage on the next to last page of the manuscript:

> *She said to bring some hot water and I could hear myself screaming now
> and I didn't care who heard and then before I knew it I heard a cry that
> wasn't my own and I was crying with it and we were crying right together.
> I saw Amelia holding it up by the hind legs and slapping it on the back
> and then she swung it around like a frog and then it let out a great cry
> and I was crying and laughing and Amelia was laughing and slapping it
> and blowing in its mouth and crying Ho! What a son! What a bastard!*

In the rewrite, attention is given to locale, "the big old warehouse
where we lived," originally owned by "a widow of the lumber maggots, we
called them," but empty now and "taken over by girls and women who

143

had no place to live." Clara lies sick in a partitioned room next to the Girl on the second floor. Amelia is there, with a "single cot" and a "mimeograph machine, which now sat in the middle of the floor." Butch's mother, driven mad by his death, is there too (she had been packed off to an asylum in the first version) and puts on a significant mad scene as the Girl awaits childbirth. A "Jesus lover" named Sara, always singing hymns, completes the entourage.

Clara's death occurs onstage just before the Girl gives birth (in the first version it is reported by Amelia). She lies dying amid a cacophony of voices: Belle crying out that there should be no more children, Butch's mother responding, "Be careful for the children, that's the future," and Sara prophesying, "Woe! woe! to the Pharisees, Herod is waiting for the little one." Of Clara it is said that she is "so tiny" and smells "like scorch or burn." The Girl, trying to get Clara to remember scenes from the Village Tavern, is joined by Amelia in a chorus of grief and anger:

> *Memory is all we got, I cried, we got to remember. We got to remember everything. It is the glory, Amelia said, the glory. We got to remember to be able to fight. Got to write down the names. Make a list. Nobody can be forgotten. They know if we don't remember we can't point them out. They got their guilt wiped out. The last thing they take is memory. Remember, Amelia says, the breasts of your mothers. O mama help us now. (126)*

Clara finally dies, her mouth "in an awful O shape as if her last breath hurt" (128). The women dress her for her funeral, in a white dress "like a bride's with lace," with "a high neck that covered the bruises" of shock therapy (129). Amelia calls for a mass meeting to protest Clara's death—"We accuse. Yes, we point a finger" (130)—and the women assemble to produce a leaflet on the mimeo machine standing in the middle of the floor. They make "a little cave" for the Girl's birthing, and Amelia assists in the delivery, as she did for Belle's cat at the beginning of the book. As the Girl begins to deliver, the mimeograph machine starts up, churning out the leaflet for the memorial meeting for Clara. The birthing scene is remarkably different from the first version:

> *I felt all the river broke in me and poured and gave and opened. Was it my cry, the cry of the women, the cry of a child? The last breath of Butch, the first of a child. Covered with a kind of slime and dark she lay the child on me. A girl, she cried, a girl, and she rubbed the slime and the child let a little gasp and breathed and before my eyes turned and glowed the dark memory, flushing. She turned golden as Clara, even her wet hair.*
>
> *Belle was shouting, It's a girl, and the women murmured happily, It's a girl!*
>
> *A woman, Amelia cried, still wiping the body with her hands.*
>
> *Belle was shouting, and for a moment the mimeograph stopped then*

began again.
*It's a woman, Belle was shouting, a sister a daughter. No dingle
dangle, no rod of satan, no sword no third arm, a girl a woman a mother.
Amelia cried, Ho ho, a new woman.
Light, I said, Claro Clara.* (131)

III.

Meridel's effort in writing *The Girl* was all uphill, from the beginning to
the rewrite efforts of 1977 and 1978. She was a rare woman's voice among
the preeminent writers of the early Communist movement: one of the
two women attending the American Writers Congress of 1935, and one
of very few to work in the proletarian fiction genre. (One thinks of Tillie
Olsen, Myra Page, and Josephine Herbst as the other successful practi-
tioners.) And *The Girl* in its manuscript version of 1939 met with mixed
responses. while her friend and rank-and-file Communist comrade Irene
Paull was deeply moved by it, the famed Communist orator Elizabeth
Gurley Flynn warned her that the book was politically incorrect, with
"lumpen tendencies," and wished it had shown "virtuous Communist
women" instead of "degenerates" such as Clara. Some of Meridel's report-
age which formed the raw material for the book had been printed in the
left magazines of the day, but one such piece, "Women on the Breadlines,"
drew a critical response in print from the editor of *The New Masses* (Whit-
taker Chambers, of all people) to the effect that it was "defeatist in attitude"
and "lacking in revolutionary spirit and direction."

Nor was Meridel better supported by the commercial end of the publishing business. Despite the efforts of her agent Maxim Lieber, the manuscript of *The Girl* was returned by a New York publisher who claimed that
the gangster sequences especially were "unrealistic." Lying just beneath
that claim was the presumption that a woman could not write about such
matters accurately. Also, the prudery of the day dictated discretion in treatment of sexual scenes and hard swearing. Some of the most obvious filling
in of linguistic "gaps" in the revised version come with the new, overt
sexual descriptions and the arrival of swearwords previously omitted. (When
I have taught the book, I have had students in Kansas refuse to study it
because of references to the male sex organ and "the taking of Christ's
name in vain.")

When it came to the rewrite, Meridel had less difficulty. It was, after
all, the encouragement of a new generation of readers which helped her
to see the new literary works into existence. But there were perhaps more
subtle pressures: I must report her frequent remark that, while she loved
the nurturing she had received from the "new generation of women," she
despaired at times over the blindness and lack of a sense of history of writers coming out of what she called, in characteristically left rhetoric, the
"petty bourgeois women's movement." Meridel could not explain her
Marxist understanding of dialectical form in the novel to feminists any
better than she could explain her "Indian" and feminist understanding of

"writing in a circle"—challenging the "linear" male novelistic form—to Marxist or male readers. Her efforts to explain herself were, I now think, nothing short of heroic.

In her rewrite of *The Girl*, Meridel did not, I think, replace a Communist vision with a feminist one, as some have claimed, or elevate the idea that the "personal is political" into a literary creed. Her ideas on literary technique, expressed in 1980 in the revised pamphlet *Worker Writers*, retain a Marxist flavor; and her sense of relationship to the women of the thirties, expressed in the 1977 preface to the pamphlet *Women on the Breadlines*, remains as much a left statement as it is a feminist one.

To properly understand Meridel's intention, it must be emphasized on the one hand that *The Girl* is about real women, some of whom still survive today in Minnesota sanatoriums, all of whom were caught up in the poverty of the Midwest depression. The Communist organizer Amelia is also drawn from life, as traces of her ethnicity, especially in the first version, attest. Yet the intent of the depiction of these "real women" is always deeply political. In both its versions, the novel is written more to teach and to move to action than to show "real" characters in a setting. What has changed in the second version is that Meridel has entered into a new *kind* of political action: She has opened up a view of woman's experience with which to confront the political dialectic of the earlier time. Alongside class analysis, she has instituted a kind of natural feminism which interrogates the Communist framework of the early manuscript with the intention of opening up a new dialectic. How else are we to explain the fact that, to this day, Meridel has not lost the thread of connection to the American Communist movement, any more than she has "abandoned" the women's movement? By Communists as well as by feminists, she is widely admired, though not always, I think, wisely understood.

Finally, a personal note. As I pause now to look back over the 1977–78 revised manuscript of *The Girl*, replete with typographical errors, due partly to the tiny portable typewriter she was working on and partly to her slow recovery from a numbing stroke, I remember Meridel's immense courage, and I feel moved and honored to have worked with her, to have inhabited the same earth and breathed the same air. She has always been a remarkable embodiment of her own optimistic dream for the betterment of all of us. May her work survive to see interpretations worthy of her spirit.

—Albuquerque, 1987

THE STORY AND THE LIVING: Meridel Le Sueur's *The Girl*

by Joseph Napora

Memory is all we got, I cried, we got to remember. We got to remember everything. It is the glory, Amelia said, the glory. We got to remember to be able to fight. Got to write down the names. Make a list. Nobody can be forgotten. They know if we don't remember we can't point them out. They got their guilt wiped out. The last thing they take is memory. Remember, Amelia says, the breasts of your mothers. O mama help us now. (The Girl, 126)

The book is in essence conflict (not always opposition), not only because change and process are conflict but because Meridel Le Sueur's *The Girl*, written in 1939, is still not settled into any comfortable stasis within the literary tradition. The true classics never do, or never remain there long. *The Girl* is not a classic. An unknown classic is a contradiction of the language. That it will become a classic is in doubt only if our literature is in doubt.

The question is not will we fail to recognize the worth of this novel but whether we will fail to establish that larger tradition within which this novel will find a place of worth. It will not become a classic because of any critical attention (this essay is not propaganda for it). But because of its influence on readers and writers and because of their influence on the culture that has up until recently effectively kept it hidden, it is classic.

In other words, the novel has the chance of being accepted within the tradition if the tradition is recovered and seen anew. But this larger conflict is not my immediate concern, even though it cannot be ignored that the past critical betrayal of *The Girl* is an indictment of the literary establishment—meaning the critics and reviewers not all of whom are academics but who have distorted the aesthetic judgment so that any work is pronounced flawed that has the possibility of altering the society's status quo.

I am intrigued by *The Girl* for several reasons, but the main one—the one that draws me back to successive rereadings—is the story. It is the story that has been denied us until now. *The Girl* helps rescue from oblivion a significant portion of our language. This story, like all true stories, continues to inform us now. This is one reason why Le Sueur is a heroine to a large and growing number of female readers. But considering gender as the issue does not reveal the main significance of the story, nor is it primarily developed along class lines. The story is significant now because the way it was told—how form and content are not separable—becomes a model for a renewed literature that puts the lie to the prevailing aesthetic prejudice that an art of the people is necessarily simplistic.

It is the internal complexities of *The Girl* that reveal the worth of the characters because of the novel being true—in a way very few novels that attempt realism have ever been true—to the story of those characters. In her afterword to the West End Press edition of *The Girl* Le Sueur explains how various essential parts of the story were given her by her friends who lived them. The story is a collective, then, instead of solely the artist's imposition of the tyranny of the imagination. It is her being faithful to the dynamics of the people's stories that has kept process and conflict integral to the artistry—and hence recognizable—and hence true.

BOOYA

> *Ganz asked for you. He wants you to bring him his Booya.* (3)

Women as meat. This is not a revelation. *Playboy* magazine successfully demonstrates it. Only a woman, however, could tell us how pervasive is the identification. In this, then, Le Sueur is sectarian. But it is a sectarianism born from love, not from the impulse to divide and conquer. The fact that a man could not reveal all of these identifications should move us to give thanks that this woman has done so.

> *Stirring the Booya pot so it wouldn't stick, Clara said, you might find that rich guy here you know, or a movie director or a talent scout.* (1)

Making the woman into a whore in her own mind to feed the man with her body.

> *. . . a pot of gold . . .* (1)

(If so, what is the rainbow? Can it be how a woman can see herself? Sometimes. With support from other women.) Women as money. Of course. But most of all a thing to consume. Meat.

> *O, Clara was so pretty with a little heart-shaped face and a white soft skin she greased every night.* (1–2)

> *[Belle] . . . so big, with dyed red hair and white skin.* (2)

> *[Clara] Anyhow, kid, she said. I think I'm getting used to looking. I can't speak to 'em like I used to when they thought they was getting chicken.* (51)

> *[the Girl] What would we eat? I said. I'd eat you, Butch said. You're sweet.* (61)

Women as meat is only one aspect of this society's need to turn us all into objects; but it is made explicit and can be seen even without a defined ideology when that act infects all relations between women and men, women and mothers, women and women.

Emily (the Girl's mother) trades a handmade rug for a sheep so her family can eat.

> *It's a fierce feeling you have for your husband and children like you could feed them your body, and chop yourself up into little pieces. The stew boiled over, sizzled. . . . Ah, what a meal.* (36)

> *. . . opened the shed door and there it hung straight from its two feet tied together and the place bleeding where I had cut out a piece for stew.* (35)

[Butch] All right, let your blood out, open the gates! (42)

[the Girl] I read all the sandwich signs american cheese, chickenham-porkcoffeemilkbuttermilklettucetomatohotbeef. They looked like signs like lovehatejealousymarriage. (43)

[Butch] My God, he said, there's blood on the sheet. You're bleeding. (46)

The woman as sacrificial lamb. Again, this is not new. Not invention. And because it is not, it is all that much more powerful as more is revealed to us. Le Sueur is not inventing things to stimulate our imagination; she is revealing back to us what we already know, in fact what we— that larger thing we aspire to, a community—have told her. Her artistry is to tune the language so that it reveals meaning at every turn, where every turn can effectively move us. It is because of this possibility for moving that a world of difference exists between a crude joke that identifies a carrot with the cock and the scene Le Sueur presents. That difference is art because of the faith she maintains in language as a bond common to us all.

If she don't feel good, Belle hooted. Never mind, the first time is the hardest and when is the last time? Put more carrots in, Amelia, I got all those horse carrots at the market, they're strong but good. (47)

The Market. The marketplace. Stock market. Prostitution. The endless reverberations of a common theme when the writer opens herself up to these stories.

Woman as meat. But this is not, cannot be, an isolated theme. Intimate to it is the denial of a woman's true story. Le Sueur, in the writing of *The Girl*, gives us that story. But she also records the loss of countless other stories.

And directly connected to that loss is abortion. Again, recurring in another guise—woman as meat. Belle:

My luck, the first time and I got into trouble. He gave me a little money and I come to St. Paul where for ten bucks they'd stick a huge vet's needle into you and start it and then you were on your own. I tell you many farm girls died in the slaughterhouses of St. Paul. I was lucky it came out that night and I wrapped it in a copy of the St. Paul Dispatch *and threw it in the river.* (47–48)

The theme is directly stated when the character needs to be explicit to reveal it to herself to ward off the assault of that theme each day. Amelia:

They get your blood and bones one way or another, What are we? Just goods to be bought and sold? Yes, she answered herself cursing, that's what they think, buy and sell you and then use your body after you're dead! It's too bad, it's too bad they can't kill our babies and eat them like suckling pigs. What tender meat that would be! Stuffed babies with mushrooms. Why not? (120)

This explicit use of the language is just one aspect of the language that has been denied us in our literature. What has been considered as progressive and avant garde has usually been merely a liberal promotion of the market system that quickly turned "obscenity" into a commodity. Effective language, language of change, has been kept hidden. And the effect on our literature has been worse for that. The literature has been impoverished because the stories have been distorted. The distortion has also been to benefit the artists most firmly entrenched in the existing market system— whether it be the commercial or academic markets. The results have been the same—only the male story gets told. The female becomes merely the muse. Woman as meat to feed the (predominantly male) artist.

> *[Amelia] They stuff you up with fine words and then they stick you in the stomach like a pig.* (120)

CATS

Booya is woman-meat. Cats is man-thing. Cats is also symbol. But most of all it is man—man made thing. Feeding on meat.

> *Booya. It's an elegant stew of chicken and veal and beef and every kind of vegetable and you cook it all night and all day very, very slow and it gets to smelling even out on the street and the cats look in the window.* (1)

Voyeurs. Peeping Tom-cat-ism. The back-alley man. Alley cats.

> *Clara told me all about what was going on up there and it scared me—the men who came in the back alley door and went past the bar and upstairs scared me.* (1)

> *And Clara would take my place when Belle told me to take them beer, because she could "field" them better when they tried to make a home run or a stirke with their too-free paws.* (1)

It is not surprising to see men portrayed as beasts. What is surprising, because it is so rare a thing, is the sympathy and the refusal to make the too easy comparisons. Cats is also woman.

> *I liked to see Belle at the bar shaking dice and the big cat Susybelly in a big bow by the register, with a piggy bank beside her full of money from the bets being put down on how many cats she would pop.* (2)

Cats is woman turned by man into a thing.

> *Clara said, Look at that now. Cats get better care than humans. She got a cup of milk a day.* (6)

Then later, Clara forced into shock therapy. Mind gone but body still starved for milk. The women rally making milk for Clara the issue. The Hearst Milk Fund is a recurring bad joke. Readers looking for a literature that redeems itself through irony will get more than enough irony though little redemption. Redemption is harder to realize. It comes through values outside of the inner complexities of the novel. It comes through working for changing the cause of the need for irony.

The cat-as-woman identification points to the larger theme of birth—birth against a system that imposes death. This is the difference between this identity and the other, cats-is-men. Amelia sees the necessity for the identification because she sees through but beyond the immediate social concerns.

> *She's a female like us, Amelia said. She don't know the father. She gives all she's got to make them come out whole healthy full of seed.* (6)

The hope for the future. It is this living thing posed against the constant attempt illustrated by cats-is-man to stifle and control it that gives these symbols a dynamism seldom seen in our literature.

Once again the issue becomes "Who controls the story, and why?" We know who has controlled it in the past. Thankfully this is changing somewhat. But even now the issue is still language. Man is cat/controller/eating, as opposed to woman is cat/giver/birthing.

The gangster offers money for a "piece" of the girl. To buy her out to shut (plug) her up.

> *Ganz said, Jesus what a coat. You could have a good coat. Cat got your tongue?* (56)

BASEBALL

> *Tragically frightened, men fear authentic relationships and even doubt the possibility of their existence. On the other hand, fearing solitude, they gather in groups lacking any critical and loving ties which might transform them into a cooperating unit, into a true community. "Gregariousness is always the refuge of mediocrities," said Nikolai Nikolaievich Vedeniapin in Dr. Zhivago. It is also an imprisoning armor which prevents men from loving.* (Paolo Freire, *Education for Critical Consciousness*)

Baseball is a man's game and a man's entertainment. A sport that quickly turns the living drama into numbers where each player is ranked into a hierarchy modeling the paternal business ordering that is the reality called "progress."

There are many types of progress. Some include time in an authentic enlargement of opportunity based upon the past struggles of people—hence, the realization that personal sacrifice for the benefit of others is not a deception. The other kind of progress, the dominant kind in our culture, feeds on the illusion of bettering the lot of everyone to the real enrichment of the few. The push of modern medical research for such practices as heart transplants utilizing funds for community health is only one of the more pronounced and pathological examples. More to the point of this story is the association of baseball with progress up the social ladder. Baseball equals making it. And making it means accepting, and promoting, the kind of competition that insures that for someone to progress, others have to be walked over.

Progress is the underlying mythos of the capitalist system which demands expansion, because without it, it will die. To insure its own survival, especially in periods when it is nearly fatally sickened, the promotion of the myth of progress is virulent. And although big business is the spokesman for the myth, it knows that internal cooperation guarantees its success if it can also confuse its potential opposition.

It is fitting then that the character who completely accepts the idea of progress is the ex-ballplayer, Butch. Butch who dies after being shot while robbing a bank—trapped within the slave mentality of unquestioningly accepting an idea that destroys him. Butch the robber. Not like Ganz the gangster and petty capitalist. Nor is he an outlaw who understands the system and inadvertently fights against it. He is just a desperate robber-to-be and ex-ballplayer living in illusions that only benefit a society bent on using, discarding, or killing him.

> *We're natural winners. You should have seen us playing ball. Our old man didn't want us to play on Sundays. We used to pray that ball right over home plate. I used to say to that ball, Go on baby do good.* (5)

Baseball as business as religion. The militant Calvinists who infused capitalism with justification from god couldn't have invented a more appropriate game.[1]

Assuming that Butch is baseball is capitalism and that capitalism must expand to survive, what is Butch's hope for the future?

> *Gee, honey, I'm crazy about you, you're so sweet. We'll have some land, we'll get you fat with roses in your cheeks and then we can have that ballplayer, fat and sassy.* (13)

No longer "only" a person, Butch is baseball—

> *Well, you're looking at me, he said, the handsomest ballplayer in the league ain't that so boys?* (68)

But so is every man in the novel. They are all joined in this fake community, this mere gregariousness (ain't that so boys?) that keeps them united on a superficial level to substitute for a unity that will threaten the economic system. Butch's brother is also a ballplayer. And it is the two of them who get jobs as scabs. And the brother is killed in the riot resulting from the attempt at strike-breaking. And then there is Joe, the Girl's brother, whose language is not even his own, so completely has the process of dreaming and subservience undercut his ability to act.

> *Mama, if I was a millionaire I'd take you on a spree, I'd buy you some candy and crackerjacks I don't care if we never get back.* (33)

This is not, however, a fatalistic picture. One time the identification of baseball and progress is shown to be a way of genuine advancement. It is within a community struggle for and with each other.

> *[Belle] Kid you should have seen the demonstration, hundreds outside the courthouse and the cops threw tear gas out the windows and some of those ballplayers caught the bombs and threw them right back and kid you should have seen those bureaucrats, like rats, pouring out of the building and the street littered with those leaflets saying Milk and Iron Pills for Clara.* (129)

The difficulty, realizing the opposition and then realizing just who it is you are playing the game for, how to transfer those skills for your own liberation, is that the language has been debased. Since she is a woman, the Girl cannot completely enter into the man's specially coded language since it excludes her and hence denies them a source of strength that could save them from themselves.

> *Had Butch won, struck a foul, thrown a home run, made the bases or struck out? How could you ever know?* (47)

The Girl does not finally need to know because she has not been as thoroughly victimized by the distortion of her language. With Butch it has become complete. So much so that it is a flaw, and a flaw we all suffer under to varying degrees, that makes Butch a tragic character (and which expresses some of the qualities that name this a tragic age). Butch never learns. His total acceptance of progress has undone him. As he bleeds to death he says:

> *Where are we going? It's got to show soon. What are we looking forward to? You got to believe in the future.* (90)

THE PHILOSOPHY OF BEATING

(When America's greatest revivalist preacher, Billy Sunday, entered New York on April 7, 1917, the day after the U.S. declared war on Germany, it was the occasion of his greatest triumph. He was to play to his biggest crowds, bigger than the ones that had cheered him at the Polo Grounds during his baseball playing days. Sunday had an immense popular following but had been used so often by the businessmen and government officials to confuse the workingmen and divide the people that he was in great demand as a strike-breaker or to be used to whip up the people for an expansionist war frenzy. He once, for instance called for a march on Mexico. But this time he was in New York to help the American war effort, solidify friendships, and most of all to become a living legend. When he exited from the train at Grand Central Station he walked over to J.D. Rockefeller and put his hand around his shoulders and said, "Hello old chap!")

For Butch, for the revivalist, for the capitalist, the world is a ball. Something to be manipulated for their own personal end. Each has accepted and promoted the conjunction of religion and business. For the capitalist the world is a neutral object to be made meaningful through treating it as a commodity infused with value by transformation of the material into something to sell. The revivalist seeks transformation of the matter into the equally abstract moral value that he can control. Butch, the confused would be petty-bourgeoisie—always looking to have a gas station of his own to manage—baseball was his only personal transformation, his only realization of success: a success that is after all so similar to the other two in that it approximates a rape, this need to be "on top of the world."

> *I like to beat everybody in the world. . . . Sure, beating's everything. Everything there is. Do you know winning is better than anything, than anything at all. When I used to play baseball I liked to beat. I was a good player. Jesus, my old man didn't want me to play baseball on Sunday. I used to pray to that ball, yeah man, I'd pray. I used to say to that ball, go on baby, do good! Yes, I got to be better than anybody, better than anybody at all. When you play ball you pray, that's the way I pray now, to be better than anybody. When you play ball you pray, those balls come over on the inside and connect. That's what I'm going to do. Let it come to me world, and connect.* (14)

The philosophy of beating is the cult of the individual. It marks, more than anything else does, the difference between the men and women in *The Girl*. Men are the individualists, the rugged capitalists modeled on the robber baron image. Women are cooperaive, the emerging socialism, and an image of a primitive tribalism. In *The Girl* the conflict is between *balls* and *eggs*.

> *It takes guts, he said, that's what it is, to go through the night. You got to be tough and strong alone.*
>
> *I don't like it alone, I said. I don't want to be alone. I want to be with others.*
>
> *He looked at me. Gee, women are funny eggs, he said, my mother's a screwy dame too!* (15)

The incompatibility of balls and eggs is shown best in the language Butch uses when the Girl becomes playful. The slightest threat to the pathological type of masculinity that Butch has adopted has him react to the Girl's spontaneity by turning her from a "sister" to a whore.

> *You egged me on, he said, you got me going, now it's your fault. You got to take the consequences. I was surprised.*
>
> *You got to take your medicine, he said, you egged me on. You did it on purpose. You got me riled up now. You can't say I wasn't treating you like a sister and then you jumps out of the car and runs like a harlot.* (24)

It is in his attitude toward women and in his unquestioning acceptance of the myth of making it in America, which amounts in practice to the same thing, that Butch becomes the Girl's father becomes Ganz becomes every male figure either trapped or using his limited power to subjugate women. It is the attitude that denies Butch sisterhood with women.

[Stasia, on the Girl's father] He wanted to be king, to boss, she said. Because he was a failure he wanted others to be so that they wouldn't be better than him. (31)

He beat me before people. Now he'll never beat me again. I'm glad he's dead. (31)

[the Girl dreaming] I didn't want to sleep, I dreamed about it every night. It was Butch in the grave instead of papa and they would both be after me to beat me up and mama would hide me. (39–40)

It seems always to return to this. The story. And who should tell it. Who can tell it truly. And who has been preventing them from telling it.

[the Girl] I didn't feel good. I cried. Butch got mad and slapped me. (45)

I remember my father always in anger, putting on his pants, leaving, yelling obscenities and coming back later, drunk, when he often beat mama, and it didn't sound too different from love-making. (45)

Instead of answering he struck me full in the face. . . . (75)

Don't Butch, I whispered, someone will see. I could see his hand lifted, this time in a fist and it struck me in the mouth. . . . (75)

If the Girl is the potential writer, the possible teller of stories, what kind of stories can she write? Who will they be written for? And why? Much of this is answered in the very writing of this novel, but what is certain within the novel itself is that the Girl will not be bent to serve the market system that is attempting to destroy her. Momentarily confused, she sells herself thinking it the right thing to do, the only thing that will guarantee Butch's love for her, then she realizes the full extent of what she has risked.

I saw the ten dollars. I reached up and Hone put his hands around my waist.
    I felt like somebody was hitting me on the top of the head with a mallet driving me into the earth, driving me deep down and I would never see anything more but darkness. . . .
    Ganz suddenly brought his huge mutilated hand back and struck me full in the face. (62)

SISTERHOOD

I wanted to find Belle and Amelia and Clara and my mama. (47)

After giving herself to Butch and realizing he had nothing to give her except the baby forming inside her, which was not given but which she unknowingly took from him, she turns for help to those able, in spite of all, to give it.

Leave her alone, Belle said.
    No, Amelia says, nobody is alone. I'm glad you came here if you don't

feel good. (47)

(When do you know when to stop analyzing? I look at this fragment and see a skill whether deliberate or unconscious, "natural," that uses the past tense "said" to imply not only Belle's character, her partial acceptance of sisterhood and her partial acceptance of domination under Hoinck, but also to show in contrast with Amelia's "says" that the attitude of leaving each other alone is no longer possible, the belief and the acting on the belief that *no one is alone* is ongoing, is present tense.)

> *[Amelia] Why, she said, you will have a child and then you will belong to the whole earth.*
> *I looked at her. She was the first person who seemed to be glad of it. I feel lonely, I said.*
> *Oh stuff, she cried, why you aren't alone now, she laughed.* . . . (99)

It is obvious that the philosophy of beating is the philosophy of capitalism. Men embody that philosophy. But *The Girl* is not so naive a story as to draw the lines between men and women so firmly based on such a simplistic analogy.

I do not know what Meridel Le Sueur's connection is with Marxism. I suspect that her brand of socialism would find little favor in the Soviet Union, though probably not as little as has been shown her by the official so-called culture in her own country. The cooperative attitudes displayed in *The Girl* seem more a realization of an intuitive tribalism than anything based on rigid systems.

> *Amelia said, It isn't the man. A man is a mighty fine thing, there is nothing better than a man. It's the way we have to live that makes us sink to the bottom and rot.* (100)

The system. If Marxism can help to bring down that system, then Marxism. But there is something more basic, more positive, more spiritual, than any western philosophy, which all are basically philosophies of beating, that seems to inform Le Sueur's work. I am thinking now of how the attack on the women in *The Girl* parallels the attempt by the government to kill the American Indian culture by sterilizing women—attacking fertility itself. Under the guise of liberal concern about overpopulation, it is a continuing policy of genocide begun at Plymouth over three hundred years ago.[2]

Le Sueur's fundamental theme of the need for women to retain their fertility, to continue the process of birth, and through that process "belong to the whole earth," puts her more in the membership of the Pequots who first resisted the European invasion than in any European sectarian group.

> *Miss Rice came in and smiled. Maybe if she hadn't smiled it would have been all right. Maybe if she hadn't said, I'm your friend, it's just between us. Maybe if she hadn't handed me that paper right at that mo-*